THE HEART OF REIKI

Richard Ellis

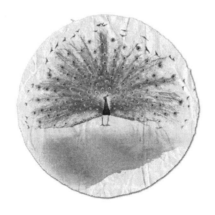

For information on the author's workshops,

please go to

www.practicalreiki.com

CONTENTS

ACKNOWLEDGMENTS

It is to the earth and the heavens that I owe my greatest thanks and the vast plains of Africa where I took my first steps. It is to the twists and turns of life's journey that has shaped and molded me and it is to those that I have been privileged to share it with along the way. In my journey through life I have been supported by a great number of people - my family, friends, teachers, students and clients.

Of particular importance I thank my immediate family who lived with me whilst I wrote this book. My Magda, for her unconditional love and support, maintaining an even keel and keeping me focused on the goal. My children, Maya, Sammy and Kimi who are my breath and keep my feet firmly planted on the earth.

To those who believed in me and through who's generosity this book was made possible; Peter and Sue Ellis, Erica Bensly, Rob Downer, Jane Morgan Jones, Jackie Fletcher, Marc Lallemand and David Parrish.

To Paul Young for his friendship, inspired artwork, creativity and ability to work long into the night for little reward.

To Caro Ness for her ability to edit my work with sensitivity, her encouragement, positive feedback and emotional support.

To Donna and Cheryl for volunteering to model for me and helping to make the book look so beautiful.

To my mother for all her proof reading and encouragement and my father for always being such a huge support, I love you guys.

Elizabeth Latham who reminded me that in spite of great distance we are always connected. For her dedicated research, unwavering loyalty to Hawayo Takata and for generously sharing information and photos.

To Paige Pixel at thepixelatedpen.com for generously allowing me to run his 'Tale of MalekTaus' on page 4/5 of this book.

Carrie, Michael and Olin for sharing the magic and letting me write our story.

David Parrish for his caring friendship, knowledge, guidance and support on every level. Babe Bensly and Dave Mac for their generosity and loving friendship.

To Mari Suehiro for her help with Japanese translations, Katie Light for her encouragement and feedback and Eloise Draper 'the word wizard' for her help with formatting. Clara Apollo for the L'Homme Terrestre Naturel and Caroline James for the Ted Kaptchuk connection.

To Pam Gregory for giving me a nudge.

To my friends Jane, Angie and Ali for being there and understanding what it is to truly support another human being.

To the memory of Richard Buckley, Belinda Clarke, Sabrina Tamborini and Debbie Taylor. I miss you with all my heart.

To the river Stour and my trusty canoe for teaching me it's easier to flow with the tide than paddle against it.

Finally to all those who have undertaken their healing journey with me as their guide, it has been a privilege to serve you. To all my Reiki family who's continued support and enthusiasm for this book has been a constant motivation. To my Reiki master June Woods for the gift of Reiki and to Hawayo Takata for leading the way.

Thank you.

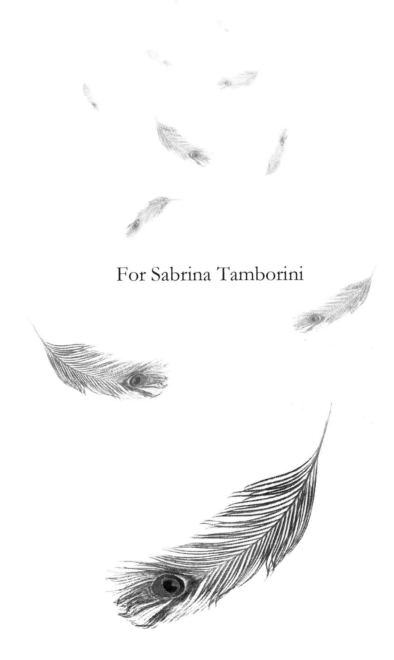

For Sabrina Tamborini

INTRODUCTION

*"Forget not that the earth delights to feel your bare feet
and the winds long to play with your hair".*

Kahlil Gibran

There is something valuable to be learnt from letting go into the flow and putting our trust in the universe. When we truly surrender and allow the universe to participate in our lives, wonders occur. We learn to follow our own internal compass, sense which way to go, recognise the signposts being offered as clues and listen to the messages being given to us. It's as if when we truly surrender, the whole universe conspires to support us.

When I first felt the inner call to write again, I was told to create space, let things go and stop everything I was doing for a while. Not an easy task when so many relied upon me in so many different ways. I was sitting on the beach looking out at the sea when I finally decided to heed the call. I remember saying inside of myself "OK, I will do it" and feeling the full potential of that decision as, suddenly, an overwhelming sense of energy and joy filled me. Then my mind asked the question; "How are you going to support the family if you don't work for 5 months?" I had no idea, I didn't even know exactly what I was going to write, I just knew I had to create the space to do so.

As is often the way when we surrender and allow the universe to inspire our actions, what came through was for me another level of understanding about the Reiki system. I allowed the seed of an idea to germinate and as I dived deeper into the relationship between Shamanism and Reiki and looked at the etymology, I started to see connections and clues to the system that Mikao Usui had constructed. I realised more than ever before that Reiki was not just an energy healing practice that can be administered to another, but for those that seek it, a profound spiritual path for self development as well.

I followed the trail of spiritual concepts and practices that had migrated across eastern Asia. In particular, I looked at how ancient Taoist and Qigong practices may have influenced Mikao Usui the founder of Reiki. I also wanted to share what I had learned in all the years of my own practice, what had worked for me, what was valuable. My intent with the book was to echo my intuitive approach to healing and allow Reiki to inform me and take me in whatever direction it wanted to go. That way I reasoned as I allowed the book to unfold and come through me I would learn. As I did, my own relationship to this beautiful practice that has been the mainstay of my life since 1993 deepened.

Within the Reiki system are encoded ancient archetypes that through their relationship to one another, connect us back in time via an evolutionary trail, to the highest antiquity. It is said Reiki is not affiliated with any one religion, which for many is part of its appeal. However within the Reiki symbology, there is an ageless story that connects it to all religions of the world.

This book is about recognizing the connections between Reiki and the spiritual practices that have evolved throughout time. It is about identifying ourselves as part of the whole, intrinsically connected to the heavens and the earth. It is about the synthesis of these two opposing forces as aspects of ourselves and how they reflect the eternal interplay within the macrocosm around us. It is about what happens naturally when we surrender to these opposing forces and allow ourselves to become an empty vessel through which they can flow. It is about finding balance within and transmuting aspects of our personalities, egos and self-created identities that no longer serve us or reflect who we truly are. It is about allowing the universe to participate in our lives in every way, inform us of which directions to take and when to move.

It is about synchronicity, empowerment, responsibility, intent, inspiration, intuition and enlightenment. This book is about 'The Heart of Reiki' from its archaic roots, to its rediscovery by Mikao Usui on Mount Kurama. It is about the clues Mikao Usui left for us so that we too may discover the treasure that he found. Reiki though beautifully simple is an unfolding journey that has depths that reveal themselves when we are ready to see them. It is an opportunity for us to find our own indomitable truth. Seek clarity within the stillness and reconnect to the flow of spirit as it unfolds through us.

The ancient alchemists understood, the key to unlocking the doors of Divine Wisdom was in the integration of their spiritual and physical existence. They developed internal alchemy whereby the purification of the negative distorted aspects of one's lower earthbound self, led to reunion with the spiritual self. The alchemists believed humans full potential to become en-light-ened could only be achieved by transmuting the poisons of the mind.

The discipline of Yoga uses physical, mental, and spiritual practices to transform body and mind helping practitioners to become aware of their deepest nature. The cobra asana for example represents transformation. When the cobra is on its belly its view is limited, but when it rises up it gains perspective above the material world and realises its higher purpose.

The term Shaman has its origins in the term for the Wandering monks Shramana who renounced all aspects of security to achieve liberation. They, above all, embodied surrender and trust in the unfolding journey of life. It was as a Shramana that Gautama Buddha left his father's palace and practiced austerity. Gautama Buddha eventually recommended a "middle way", realising that integrating spirituality into physical existence was a more balanced path to walk.

With wisdom comes the understanding that we are spiritual beings and when we allow the unfolding of our universal selves, what flowers and expresses itself in physical form is our divine nature. We are not expected to renounce the physical world because to do so would be to deny part of ourselves, and the earth we come from. Instead we are to walk the middle way between our earthly self and our spiritual self and allow them to be integrated and expressed. We are part of creation's unfolding, for it is through us that consciousness evolves and knows itself.

I trust you will enjoy the journey.

Once upon a time...

Before the world grew cynical
and forgot the tales that tell the truth,
three young sisters walked the wood.
They came upon a large drab bird,
painfully gasping his last breaths,
his long neck stretched over another bird
and her smashed nest.
The eldest sister called out to the sky:
"Father, what has happened
to your child Malek Taus?"

In their hearts they heard his response:
"It's a sad tale, my children.
The emerald serpent, King Apep, charmed his mate
to slay her and devour their eggs.
Malek returned from gathering food
to find Apep's poison had already done its work
and his unborn children mere lumps
in the snake's belly. In his fury he chased Apep,
viciously attacking him even though
Malek knew he could not possibly win.

The youngest sister held the dying bird, stroking his
brown feathers, crying, "Father, he should be
rewarded, for his heart was brave and true!
Could you not grant him immunity from the poison
and set him to protect your garden?"

The middle sister said, "His beauty should match his fierce bravery. His feathers should hold all the glory of the heavens, his tail be as wide as the serpent was long."

"And you?" the father asked the eldest sister. "How would you help this creature?"
The girl considered all she had heard before answering, "My sisters' wishes are kind and good but without wisdom, beauty and strength easily become vanity and tyranny. Because you watch over your children always, into his feathers I would set a hundred shimmering eyes to remind everyone that under your gaze we should all strive to be as noble as this bird, ready to sacrifice everything for those we love."

Pleased, the father said to Malek Taus, "Rise, and accept the blessings my daughters have bestowed upon you. Go forth as my beacon, to remind people that they are stronger and braver than they know, more beautiful than they realise, and are ever protected under my watch."

And so the peacock and his mate awoke, no longer a drab brown, but bluer than the bluest sky and brighter than the most brilliant rainbow.....

BY PAIGE PIXEL

Earth's lowest point on dry land 1,401 ft below sea level

Dead
Sea

The Holy Secular Church

My story begins on a melting asphalt road
that snaked ahead through the barren
Judean desert with nothing but rock and salt either side

TRUSTING THE FLOW

"Synchronicity combined with alignment is where miracles happen.
Stay true to yourself – Be the vehicle".

Abraham

We were walking along the melting asphalt road that snaked ahead through the barren Judean desert with nothing but rock and salt either side. I was travelling through Israel with a friend from Findhorn, on our way to planet earth's lowest point on dry land 1,401 ft below sea level. It was seriously hot, the Dead Sea in July reaches upwards of 45°c, sauna like hot. The driver on the coach had warned us not to walk, but we had slept through our stop and the only way back was on foot. With only a few sips of water left, we were starting to realise the driver was right. I laughed out loud. It seemed ages ago now, but it was only this morning that I had decided to miss my flight home and head south from Jerusalem with Carrie. It was a decision that involved total commitment on my part because my plane ticket was non transferable and I didn't have enough money to get back to the UK. That morning I had experienced a powerful energy in the Holy Secular church in Jerusalem that had left me feeling incredibly centred and inwardly connected. We had sat in the sunshine afterwards and decided then that we wanted to take in the Dead Sea and head down to Elat, cross the border into the Sinai and then on down into Nuweiba. I had heard from friends in Tel Aviv, of a wild dolphin interacting with people just off the coast from a Bedouin village and it sounded good enough to tear up my return flight to Heathrow. I would leave how to get home to the great man himself. It dawned on me as we were slowly evaporating on the asphalt we would be lucky to make it to the youth hostel, never mind the Sinai! We might need the great man's help sooner than expected.

It was so quiet that the slightest sound ricocheted off the surrounding hills so we could hear the diesel struggling up the incline, long before it appeared out of the heat haze. We took our backpacks off and sat them on the edge of the road, waiting for the coach as it grew nearer so we could beckon it to stop. With an explosive hydraulic hiss, the coach announced its arrival as it came to a standstill beside us exhaling and wheezing like a mechanized bull.

The door opened; "Are you crazy people?"

The driver, cigarette clenched between grinning teeth, was perched on a large orange cushion to compensate for being a little too short to see over the steering wheel. His Ray Ban-bespectacled face was being cooled by three battery-operated fans and music was broadcasting loudly from the radio. He gestured us to get in and, after a brief debate, kindly agreed to deliver us to the youth hostel. The 30°c drop in temperature was a relief and, tripping over machine guns, we made our way to a seat thankful for heaven's intervention. I never did get used to so many Israelis carrying guns, maybe being the only person without one had something to do with it?

Having survived day one of our journey into the unknown, we took stock at the youth hostel and counted how much cash we had left. It wasn't looking great but watermelon, humus and pitta bread were cheap and we were sure we could stretch it out for at least another week! I managed to sell off a couple of youth hostel vouchers that night I had bought in Tel Aviv to two young Swiss girls. This meant we could enjoy a cold beer or two as we contemplated the next step of the adventure.

The plan was to stay in Eilat for a couple of days before heading across the border into Egypt, but as I stepped off the bus, I was filled with such revulsion for the place, I suggested we change our plan and head straight for the border. Having spent my teens in Dubai, when it was just a desert, and watched as it had slowly become a toy town, I had developed a disliking for neon signs and the so-called spoils of democracy.

After the pink and lime green Neon of Eilat, the border crossing to Taba, was like stepping through a dimensional doorway back in time. A few goats chewed on cardboard and there were some wooden benches thoughtfully scattered near huts made out of plywood which served as both the immigration offices, the bus stop and the cafe. Flies seemed to understand where they belonged and their population had increased with every step we made out of Israel. Most congregated on a mangy mutt sleeping under one of the benches, the others were buzzing around a hypnotic blue light unaware of their impending doom. With no obvious sign of what was supposed to happen next, we ordered a coke.

"Salaam Malaykum" I said, "Is there a bus to Nuweiba?" "Inshalla" said the immigration official, ticket officer and bar man with a grin! It was getting dark, so we sat down and patted mangy mutt who briefly lifted his eyebrows in recognition but was busy licking his backside and was obviously getting much more pleasure from it than we could give him!

Having finished the coke we were watching the dying embers of sunlight in the sky when we heard him, Sharm el-Sheikh, I wanna go Sharm el-Sheikh" "Yes yes, tomorrow!" says the barman.

I turned to see the silhouetted shape of a man wearing a cowboy hat standing at the bar. Whilst my eyes adjusted from staring at the sunlight, I reached out my hand and greeted him.

"Hi" I said, "You heading to Sharm el-Sheikh?"

"Yeah sure am, Michael's the name", he said. "But there's no bus till tomorrow morning!" "How about you two?"

"We are going down to Nuweiba, there's a village of Bedouins down there who have apparently made friends with a wild dolphin called Olin?"

"Is there a bus?" he asked

"Your guess is as good as mine", I say

"Tell you what, do you mind if I tag along?"

"Not at all, we would be glad of the company," I say.

The bus did show eventually and as it wound its way south, the road visible only to the driver's eyes, we had room to spread out and time to chat. I told him about Reiki, giving up London life and living in Scotland, Carrie talked of her time in Findhorn and home in Maine and Michael told us he was travelling on his own and hoping to meet up with people he knew in Sharm el-Sheikh. An hour and a half later we were in Nuweiba. The first night we stayed in bamboo huts in a beach camp and the following morning headed to Muzeina.

Not far from Nuweiba a Bedouin tribe had settled and erected a makeshift dwelling. Originally the tribe was nomadic and visited in summer to pick dates but the trade had thrived and the arrival of Olin the dolphin was attracting western visitors, so they settled. The tribe suffers from a hereditary defect and some members are born deaf mutes. Abdullah, a deaf boy, was fishing one day and the dolphin followed him home. They became firm friends swimming together every day and Abdullah named the dolphin Olin, 'a gift from God'.

Muzeina

Olin

"I will always remember those two weeks. They taught me about the unfolding adventure that is life and to trust in its flow."

Michael, Carrie and Me.

Over time, the Dolphin had a profound healing effect on many in the village. Abdullah said that swimming with Olin considerably improved his hearing. We were welcomed by big happy smiles and were taken into the water to swim with Olin.

We stayed for two weeks, getting to know the Bedouins and swimming with Olin every day. She was a great teacher, not in a deliberate sense, but just through the way of her being. She taught us how to love, how to open the heart and let joy fill us, how to let go, not be attached, and how to be playful in every moment, allowing vitality to fill our lives. She revealed our need to connect, our ego's desire to be acknowledged and special. She was so fast in her natural environment that, even with flippers, she could just play with us and be gone with the slightest movement of her tail. Ultimately we all had to accept and delight in the unique bond that Abdullah had with her.

It was incredible that even though we were in the middle of nowhere, each day someone new would turn up having heard about this magical place and the dolphin. After ten days there was a group of eight people including Michael who were interested in learning Reiki, there and then. I offered to teach everyone in exchange for the money to buy myself a ticket home. We assembled a makeshift healing room with sarongs and palm trees and performed the attunements there in front of the ocean. We exchanged treatments lying on rugs on the ground and the energy just flowed. When it got too hot we swam with Olin or rested in the shade of the palms. To celebrate our last night, the moon spectacularly rose in full from behind the Sinai Mountains and we all decided to go into the sea for a swim. Treading water with the full moon above bathing us in silver light, we joined hands forming a big circle.

From beneath us Olin rose from the depths and surfaced in the circle, clicking wildly, we gathered around her holding her in our arms giving her Reiki and she just lay there receiving… Unbelievable! If I hadn't witnessed it I would never have believed it, I was filled with so much gratitude. Then, in her customary way, she sank and disappeared into the night.

I will always remember those two weeks. They taught me about the unfolding adventure that is life and to trust in its flow. I realised that, wherever I am in the world, I have the capacity to draw to myself what I really need. Security is nice to have but not when it is at the expense of freedom and flow. Life never stays still, it is constantly moving and evolving, full of beginnings and endings.

When we become fearful of following our inner promptings because of what we might lose, we die a little inside.

Our journey into the desert taught me to have faith in the unfolding story of life. I learnt to trust my inner knowing when it made no sense to my mind and to follow the path even though it appeared to be taking me nowhere. Travelling is such a great teacher of flow, things turn up when we least expect and help us to realise how rich and abundant we really are.

PART 1.

REIKI - THE EVOLUTION AND MIGRATION OF SPIRITUAL CONCEPTS

Chi, Qi, Ki

At the very heart of Reiki, we find the theory that a vital field of energy pervades the universe.

THE UNDERLYING CONCEPTS

"The universe must be composed largely of an even more ethereal form of energy that inhabits empty space, including that which is in front of our noses".

Scientific American

At the very heart of Reiki, we find the theory that a vital field of energy pervades the universe. It is the underlying ingredient in an accepted cosmological concept in almost every Eastern country. Ki permeates and connects the Universe together, actively forming part of any living thing. Ki is the thread connecting all beings, it is present and active in all activity throughout the cosmos. The flow of Ki through countless forms is the cause and effect of the universe's unfolding story.

Ted Kaptchuk writes *"The Qi of the sun, rain and soil resonate with the Qi of the seed to bring forth a plant that already contains the germ of the plant and qualities that the sun, rain and soil touch."*

When all is allowed to flow, Ki, the active binding ingredient, creates resonance between things. The potential inherent in every thing and every situation coincides, spontaneously connecting to create the optimum opportunities for growth and development. In allowing flow we are participating in the unfolding of Creation's epic story.

It reminds me of the book, "The Magic of Findhorn", written in 1975, about the Findhorn community in Scotland. The story is about the garden that Peter & Eileen Caddy grew outside their caravan in the sand dunes of Scotland, to supplement their low income. When, at first, Peter planted seeds he was unsuccessful and so he asked his friend Dorothy McLean who meditated and communicated with the plant devas (intelligence of the plants) what was required. She was told which substances could be found on the beach and combined to create the ideal fertilizer. She was told how far apart to space plants and which plants should go next to which for the ideal resonance between them. After Peter followed the instructions, the seeds were given the ideal circumstances to grow and Peter Caddy became famous for producing huge vegetables. The growth continued beyond the garden though because soon people heard about this phenomenon and came to find out more. The inherent intelligence of Ki that connects everything together, informing people and causing situations to coincide and attract each other. Almost without effort, the seed that Peter planted and the garden he grew became an international spiritual, ecological, educational and transformational centre that thrives to this day.

My own seed of potential was stimulated and nurtured to grow at the Findhorn Foundation and this book you read is part of the ever expanding flow and flowering of that same seed planted in the ground by Peter. And on and on it will flow and unfold. A sentence here, an understanding there, and a slight shift in awareness is all that's required to realign someone to their own unfolding story. It is like a ship in the ocean making a one-degree course correction, which doesn't seem much, but after a week of sailing that ship finds itself in a completely different part of the world to where it was previously heading.

This field of energy, known as "Ki" in Japan (as in Rei-ki or Ai-ki-do) is called "Qi" in China (as in Qi-gong) or "Chi" (as in Tai-chi). In Yoga, the life energy is called "Prana" (like in Prana-yama). To avoid confusion, I will refer to it in the Japanese form Ki and Chinese form Qi & Chi depending on the origins of the philosophy I am discussing.

Ki, as a concept, has even filtered down into our mainstream culture. In Star Wars, this is the force that Obi-wan Kenobi spoke of when he said to Luke Skywalker, "May the force be with you". He taught Luke to listen to its directive and let it inform him. When he said "Use the force Luke", he suggested Luke could tap into a field of energy that would guide him to act according to its flow. Also in Japan, there is a popular animation series called Dragon Ball where the main character Goku learns to gather huge amounts of energy from the environment to create sphere's of Ki power called Genki Dama.

It has also even become de rigueur to incorporate chi philosophy into established sports. We have chi running, chi swimming, chi yoga, and chi exercise, all new approaches to old established exercise routines. These techniques teach people a flowing action in their movements, illustrating how to move with the least amount of exertion. Achieving maximum results from minimum effort is a concept that can be applied to life in general and has evolved from the Chinese philosophy of Wu Wei, (action through non action)

Wu Wei refers to the cultivation of a state of being in which our actions are effortlessly efficient and in alignment with the natural flow of our environment. It is the kind of going with the flow where we navigate from within rather than as a result of adaptation to outer stimuli and pressures. When we allow ourselves to be orientated by flow we are guided from a place of inner knowing. Keeping an eye on the destination and maintaining the flexibility to respond to changes, our actions become harmonious with our environment and for the highest benefit to all.

In nature there are clues to this principal. Water, falling as rain on a mountain top, seeks the path of least resistance as it makes its way back to the ocean. Water by its persistently fluid nature is able to find its way to its destination by flowing around obstacles too difficult to penetrate and yet can carve great valleys out of the landscape.

Wu Wei is effortless action, acting when the time is right and achieving, without the appearance of trying, which requires us to be in sync with the Universe.

'In 1993 I was at the Findhorn Foundation in Scotland going through a little realisation that the fabric of reality wasn't quite what I had thought it to be. My old paradigms were coming apart and reality was revealing itself as anything but solid.

I was running a potato peeler down the side of the biggest carrot I had ever seen in my life. As I did so, it was releasing an astonishing burst of fragrance and colour. Who would have thought peeling a carrot could form part of a mystical experience? I had been, to all intents and purposes, an emotional wreck. "Go to Newbold House", John had advised! "It's quiet there. Chop wood and carry water for a while." Karma Yoga, I found out, was the yoga of simple work; an essential ingredient in any spiritual awakening. Earlier, whilst sitting in the community gardens at the end of my stay at the Findhorn Foundation, I had needed some re assurance. It had felt as if I was looking over the edge of sanity into the void. That's when I had thought of John! A big heart of a man who had been my workshop leader during that week, he was solid and talked sense. As I had thought of him, I turned to see the minibus that ferries people into the community come round the corner and pull up in front of me. John stepped out. How is that possible I thought to myself?

Following John's advice, I spent a further week at Newbold House, only a mile down the road from the Findhorn community. It shared similar values but was like a smaller, younger version. It was there I was introduced to meditation and Qigong. I began to enjoy doing even the simplest tasks. I learnt love in action, humility and service through Karma Yoga.

My assigned jobs varied, Some mornings I would chop and stack wood, others I would work in the kitchen chopping vegetables to go in the vast aluminium pots that soups were bubbled and boiled in, their bases stained black through daily use. I meditated three times a day, lived on a vegetarian diet, sat in a sharing circle and began to integrate spirit into my life. Slowly I began to feel part of the cosmos, just like a flower bathed in sunlight that has sprouted from a branch, which is part of the tree that has grown out of the earth and the more silent and still I became, the deeper I knew it.

One of my karma free mornings, I took the bus to the Findhorn Bay. A beached tree stump that had ended its journey down the river offered the perfect perch to watch the tide roll out. It's one of those phenomena that just need to be witnessed when, like Otis Redding, you're just 'wastin time'. The bay is large and shallow and the estuary that it drains through, deep and narrow. Like a plug being pulled out of a tub, the water empties from the bay, so slowly at first, it would be imperceptible but for the boats obediently lining up like ducks in a row, as the current pulls them against their shackles. The water gains momentum, buoys bob up and down on the rippling surface, as it drains through channels etched out of the bay. Then, just like the final gurgle as the bath water disappears, with a final hurried flourish it is gone, leaving behind the disgruntled vessels unceremoniously scattered on uneven keels, as if they had fallen from the sky. Shy crabs appear out of the sandy silt sidestepping, whilst white winged opportunists riding the wind above, squawk as they look for a free seafood platter.

I never tired of watching the show but I remembered I was working in the kitchen that afternoon. I needed to be five miles away in a little less than 15 minutes. A journey, even if my name was Roger Bannister, that would take over 20. I stood up, feeling unhurried. The beauty of living in an environment where you are not the only one who has realised we are an expression of creation, is that you find yourself in the right place at the right time more frequently. It seems as if coincidence is multiplied by the number of people participating in the game. There was a certainty in what was about to happen. As I arrived by the side of the road, I heard a car approaching and stuck out my thumb. The car slowed and pulled up next to me. "Where are you heading?", she said. "I have to get to Newbold House", I replied. "No problem", she said, "That's where I am going". Ten minutes later, apron hastily tied round my back, I was peeling the fresh carrot that moments before had been plucked from the earth.'

QI, CHI, KI

UNDERSTANDING KI

"Everything is determined by forces over which we have no control. It is determined for the insect as well as for the star. Human beings, vegetables, or cosmic dust – we all dance to a mystery tune, intoned in the distance by an invisible piper."

Albert Einstein

The next couple of pages might get a little complicated as I attempt to unravel the mystery of Ki. It is the essential thread that flows through this book and I can only trust that it knows where it is heading, and that I can do it justice as I allow it to inform me. In fact, the whole of this book is an unfolding journey for the both of us, you the reader and me the narrator. I find comfort in knowing that you are reading this, as I must have found my way. I will need you to concentrate for a moment if you are going to make sense of it all.

Ki, historically, is seen as an energy but it remains immeasurable and doesn't behave as we would expect energy to from the point of view of traditional physics. This hasn't helped those trying to prove the existence of a life force. Ted Kaptchuk in his book 'The Web That Has No Weaver' suggests, Ki is not a force added to lifeless matter but rather "the state of being of any phenomena". The difficulty is that Ki, unlike light, doesn't travel in a linear way from point A. to point B. and therefore cannot be measured like energy in the traditional sense. To understand Ki we must begin to imagine everything existing in delicate balance within the same unified field. Ki is the active ingredient in any situation that causes things to connect. Viewed this way we can see Ki as the substance in the cosmos through which everything coexists.

In ancient China a model that explained the existence of the heavens and the earth was derived from the concept of a single source of energy consciousness known as Tai Yi, [the primordial unity of Yin and Yang]. It was understood everything was created from this great oneness, being part of it as consciousness and at the same time existing within it as creation. It was both the original source and the expression of that source. As long as the source existed, then the expressions of it existed. Wherever Qi accumulated like a divine spark it formed life. Each of us carries that spark within ourself like a light burning bright and when it dissipates there is death. That same spark is in everything and all of that everything floats about linked together in a great ocean-like field of Qi we call Creation. All of this everything spontaneously resonates and responds according to the active vital energy engendered in itself.

In the Tao Te Ching the primordial essence is referred to as the Dao and becoming one with this essence, to achieve effortless action, is the principle path of Taoism. The notion being that aligning ourselves to our internal Qi flow naturally aligns us to the flow of creation. It is also referred to in some texts as the Yuang Qi (Original Ki). Also Prenatal Qi, which is transmitted by parents to their children during conception. This Qi is partly responsible for a person's inherited constitution. Individually, we can connect to this ocean of Qi to increase our individual vitality and preserve our distinct divine spark, our Yuang Qi (Original Ki).

As we cultivate our relationship to this primordial essence, and listen to its rhythms, we start to align ourselves with the spontaneous rhythms of the universe, the flow. We begin to recognise and trust the voice within, our intuition, [the inner teacher]. And though we may not know where the flow is taking us it continues to pull us. By trusting and surrendering to it, our actions become aligned with a greater universal truth and we achieve what the Taoists call effortless action. As we connect and resonate with things along the way, it encourages us to continue cultivating our relationship to Qi. It's like diving into something because its depth is drawing us ever deeper.

The irony is, man searches for 'the source' by looking outwards into space and the further and further he looks into the past for a point where it all began the more he just finds infinite clouds of dust. Were he to look within he would find 'the source', is right here and we need not look very far at all, because incredibly it lives within us, we are it!

Early Alchemists referred to this Original Qi as the internal elixir. They believed that finding the secret to preserving this elixir would provide the ultimate goal of eternal life. In their attempts to prolong life, very early alchemists combined herbs and minerals to form magical life-giving potions and tinctures. Gu Qi [Grain Qi] is the nourishment derived from the digestion of food, drinks, herbs and medicines rich in Qi taken into the body.

As these ideas evolved and were perfected, two primary methods for preserving internal Qi were developed. Firstly they continued to utilise the properties of the outer Elixir found in plants, herbs and minerals, and as their understanding grew it formed the foundation of Chinese herbal medicine. Secondly, the benefits of internal energy flow practices were discovered. Initiates learned to gather and refine Qi from the heavens and the earth using meditation and breathing techniques.

They mapped out the intricate energy systems of reservoirs and channels through which Qi flowed and as a result, learned to direct Qi internally. These practices had names like "building the vessel", "readying the burner" and "the small and big heavenly circles". Ultimately it was believed that through these practices they could fulfill their goal of reconnecting with the primordial essence and experience themselves as one with the Dao.

These concepts permeated all manner of energy healing practices. A 6th Century Buddhist monk called Da Mo and more commonly known as Boddidharma is considered the first Patriach of Zen Buddhism and is believed to be responsible for the migration of many of these ideas into China. Boddidharma himself spent nine years meditating in a cave before he received 'awakening'. He created Qi enhancing exercises that formed the basis of a variety of martial arts developed in Buddhist temples throughout China.

In particular the Shaolin monks incorporated qigong and tong chi gong into their Kung Fu practice, developing the ability to gather and focus Qi energy as a form of protection. They learned to repel attacks by focusing Qi to parts of the body producing extraordinary power whilst also remaining incredibly flexible. Used correctly, they discovered Qi could make any part of the body as hard as steel, able to break bricks, sticks and stones. Today Qigong masters learn to focus and direct internal Qi outwards, creating a protective field around them known as the "iron shirt" that can repel blows to the body. In experiments, potentially lethal impacts with a baseball bat have been measured and up to 500 pounds of force have been repelled by Qi without any consequences to the Qigong masters.

KI

ETYMOLOGY

"Human beings are born because of the accumulation of qi. When it accumulates there is life. When it dissipates there is death... There is one qi that connects and pervades everything in the world."

Zhuang Zhou a 4th century Chinese philosopher

The Kanji that form the Japanese language are pictographic and, just like cave paintings, they tell a story. In order to understand the deeper meaning of the Reiki pictograph, we have to look back to its Chinese origins, where we find the archaic roots. By studying the evolution of this ancient symbolic language the hidden meanings reveal themselves to us. Qi is found amongst fragments of writings in some of the oldest texts in China.

Qi originally had the shape of rising clouds.

It later evolved to include a curling end to the top cross stroke to identify it independently from the character for the number three, 'san'.

The bottom stroke was then given a curling hook and it developed the meaning of 'clouds' or 'vapour rising' to this 'cloud-like vapour' rising and falling like our breathing.

Finally the character for rice was added to the pictograph as a representation for that which sustains and nourishes us and an association between the two characters for rice and clouds was established. This introduced a concept of nourishment and energy, giving us an interpretation for the pictograph that could mean, 'the essential substance that nourishes us like the breath'.

However if we go back further and look at the character 'Qian', from the I Ching, that represents the initiative power of Heaven [The Creative Principle], we get a possible insight into the story. Here we see an image of a rising sun radiating its light and Qi flowing out nourishing the whole world. The ancient Chinese pictograph for Qian, shown below, depicts a sun on the left side of the picture. Above the sun, there is a shoot [Rice] growing. Underneath the sun, the earth with the root of the plant penetrating deeply into the ground. On the right side, the Qi is dispersed from the sun [Like Curling Clouds] and spreads out under the sky above it.

We can see that the evolution of the pictograph for Qi has certain parallels with the character for Qian. In particular, the character for rice, reveals the yin yang balance between the heaven and earth, creating sun-like nourishment promoting growth and life. In early pictographs there was reference to Qi being like light radiating from the sun. Later, as a simplification it seems the character for sun was no longer included, leaving us with the more modern representation for Qi.

The final addition of Rice growing suggests not only the nourishment that sustains us through the food we eat, but also the light, heat and warmth of the sun being the essential vital ingredients to create life [In this case the rice shoot]. In the Qian pictograph we see the rice shoot actually growing out of the sun and at the same time sending roots into the earth as if the sun is in between heaven and earth. [We will see the relevance of this concept in our Reiki practice later]. The Qi dispersing from the sun under the sky does so like steam or curling clouds.

As well as early pictographs of Qi showing light radiating from the sun, there is also reference in older texts of light being absorbed in Qi practices from both the sun and the moon. In later chapters, we will also come to see that this is very relevant to our practice of Reiki, both in terms of an underlying concept and also symbolically.

It's interesting that throughout the world a simple form of greeting is to ask "How are you?" so many of our responses to this simple address have evolved along parallel notions of feeling connected or disconnected from energy. When we are connected we say things like; "I feel great", "I'm in the flow", "I am good", "I am full of energy" and "I am in the groove". When disconnected, we might say; "I am a bit low", "I feel flat", "I am lost, empty, exhausted and not good".

In modern Japan, Yuang Qi [Original Qi] has evolved into a colloquial form of greeting where it is pronounced 'Genki'. So when a Japanese asks "O genki desu ka?" They are asking "How are you?" When someone replies "Genki Desu", They are saying "I am in good spirits, energetic, in the groove, connected to the oneness of the universe, the primordial essence itself, Yuan Qi"! Well, they are not really, they are just saying they are fine, but you get the idea!

In Reiki training, an essential way to understand Ki is by having a tangible experience of it. Philosophising and understanding the history is all very well but to have an awareness of Ki and building a relationship to it, allows us to be informed by the energy itself and get a sense of its flow. On page 28 there is a simple exercise you can utilise to develop your awareness of Ki.

EXERCISE TO EXPERIENCE KI FLOW

Stand with feet approximately hip distance apart.
With your palms facing towards your belly begin slapping the area
vigorously with your palms. This requires no attention whatsoever but
stimulates Ki flow. Gradually begin to soften the slaps, this requires more
concentration to do it softly and becomes slightly challenging. After three
minutes begin to slap really slowly and softly. You will notice this requires
even more attention and is more challenging. Then slow down so much
that your hands are barely touching the surface of your belly. Pay attention
to what you notice about the sensations and feelings in your hands and
body. What is the temperature in your hands? Does it change as you move
your hands subtly?

Then progress by raising your arms upwards and bringing the palms of
your hands together facing each other, in front of your belly and rub the
fingertips together very gently, then draw the hands apart. Explore the
space that is created between the palms. Is it tangible? Don't try to do
anything, just simply explore what's there. Slowly draw your palms further
apart, expanding the space. What happens? Is something tangible? How
does it feel? How far can you draw your hands apart and still notice
something? What then happens when you bring your hands closer again?
Compressing the space? What do you notice? Allow your self to explore
and be led by the experience. There is nothing that should happen, you
cannot do it wrong, relax and let it flow.

If you have a partner you can explore in pairs. Set up the process as
before and then explore the space between the palms of your hands and
your partner's body. Trace around the head and down the torso paying
particular attention to the heart and stomach areas. Notice if you are
drawn to a particular spot anywhere and what happens if you just hold
your hands still over that area. Enjoy.

THE UNTOLD STORY OF REIKI

"Look, there is a spirit within your person.
Now it goes, now it comes.
No one can imagine it ....
But if you reverently clean its abode
It will come of itself.
You will recover your own true nature,
It will be fixed in you once for all."

Introduction to the shogua Stephen Karcher Ph.D.

I loved the Alchemist by Paolo Coelho. The story tells us of Santiago, a shepherd, who has a disturbing dream while sleeping under a sycamore tree. In his dream, Santiago is in a field with his sheep when a child starts to play with them. The child grabs Santiago's hands, transports him to the pyramids in Egypt, and tells him that he will find treasure there. As the child begins to say the exact location of the treasure, Santiago wakes up. He goes to a dream interpreter who insists he travels to the pyramids to find the treasure. Santiago, heads off on his journey and ultimately finds the value of his journey does not lie in the treasure at the end, but in the knowledge and experience he gains from the journey itself. The final twist in the tale is that the treasure always lay under the sycamore tree back home where the story began.

Our relationship to Reiki is an unfolding adventure that takes us on a journey. Some of those journeys are inner and some outer, as we search to find the hidden treasure. There are many who want to become masters of Reiki without taking the journey. It is a shame because there is much treasure to be found along the way, hidden in the adventure of your own unfolding story. Mikao Usui knew all along where it was buried, for he found it himself. He gave us a treasure map and clues where to dig. It is up to us, however, to gain understanding from our own unique journey and not just settle for the treasure. Just like the Alchemist said to Santiago. "There are alchemists who have lost the ability to turn lead to gold. These men, just want the treasure from their Personal Legends without actually living out their Personal Legends". So where is it buried? What is the treasure map that we have been given? And where do we need to dig? The answer of course, just like for Santiago, has lain right in front of our very eyes all along. It is found in the pictograph that forms the word Reiki itself. This simple word has so many clues about the practice and I would like to take you on a little journey through time to understand what it actually means.

In the previous chapter I introduced the Chinese concept of Yuang Qi [Original Qi]. According to Taoist theory everything is created from one energy, the primordial essence. From this single source, various different forms of Qi are emitted, like rays of light. One of them is known as 'Soul Chi', which, as I am about to show you, has very strong historical connections to the practice of Reiki.

As a teacher of both Reiki and Qigong, I have always been curious about the relationship between the two disciplines and find it fascinating that the kanji characters that form the pictograph for Reiki originated in China. The Chinese name for Reiki is Ling Chi and they share the same pictograph. Ling Chi is known as 'Soul Chi', so in essence, Reiki could also be described as soul energy.

REIKI   LING CHI

The Chinese counterpart, 'Ling Chi' describes the spiritual energy that envelops and forms all things. It is believed by practitioners of Qigong that before we can connect with and perceive the 'Ling Chi' contained within the cosmos and our environment, first we must cultivate our own personal Ling Chi. Through the cultivation of stillness and emptiness within, we begin to feel the rhythms and flow of internal Qi. As we become more aware of this internal Qi we can feel where restrictions to its flow occur.

Through practice we begin to cultivate, gather and refine Qi within, and learn to direct its flow. As we develop in awareness we recognise our intimate connection between Earth and Heaven. Slowly we open and surrender to the external universal flow of Qi and allow it to direct our movements and lives.

I will now break down the Kanji characters in turn and reveal to you the story that is Reiki. The pictographs for Reiki, Ling Chi and Qigong share certain characters which, when combined, have different meanings. I will begin with the kanji for gong, which is common in all three pictographs.

Gong is a pictograph of a simple tool carpenters used for measuring, an ancient T-square. It is also the scepter-like instrument seen in the hand of the Goddess Nuwa who, according to Chinese mythology, created humankind.

GONG 'SKILL'

'Gong' is used to describe the 'cultivation, attainment or development of something. Just like the carpenter is required to master his skills to fashion something out of wood, Gong relates to developing skills through practice, time, discipline and hard work'. It also stood for order, correct behaviour and the law of nature. It is found in the pictograph of Qigong with the addition of the character Li, which means 'power or strength' and Qi, which, as we have learnt already, means 'life force'.

QIGONG

Qigong then can be interpreted to mean in a fairly long-winded way 'The attainment of skill and mastery through researching the practices and disciplines related to Qi.' Simply it means, 'the practice of cultivating life force.' In the Huangdi Neijing [Classic of Medicine] Gong means doctor and we know ancient Chinese doctors evolved from shamanistic traditions. In the carpenters square found in our ling chi pictograph we have extra characters that turn the character 'Gong' into the character for 'Wu', which literally means Shaman. The image below shows the older character on the left as you look at it.

WU 'SHAMAN'

32

Wu refers to the work of sorcerers and mediums. It is synonymous with the magician in the Tarot deck who takes the power of the universe and channels it through his own body and directs it to the physical plane. The magician has his right hand raised to the heavens and his left pointing to the earth and he acts as a bridge between the two realms. The magician, like the alchemist and the shaman, harnesses the primordial elements of earth, air, fire and water. Above his head is the symbol of infinity representing no limitations; everything to him is possible, when he is open to the flow of the universe.

Shamanism is a practice that involves reaching altered states of consciousness in order to encounter and interact with the spirit world and channel these transcendental energies into this world. A shaman is a person regarded as having access to, and influence in, the world of benevolent spirits, who can enter into trance states during rituals and practice divination and healing. The shaman is seen as someone who can bridge the gap between heaven and earth. Who can conjure up the elements, harness the power of creation, talk to the ancestors and call upon and embody the power of Great Spirit.

Shamanism is a worldwide phenomenon found in cultures on every continent throughout the world. Shamans acted as intermediaries or messengers between the human world and the spirit worlds. Shamans looked to spirit for the solutions to problems afflicting the community. They believed the cause of illness lay in the afflictions of the soul. Restoring balance and harmony resulted in the elimination of the problem.

During the Yin Kang period of Chinese history, shamans or the Wu incorporated dancing and chanting into their healing rituals. Dance was the method of invoking and connecting to the primordial essence and Original Qi. Researchers have theorised that Qigong originated from the shamanic dances of early Wu shamans. The additional characters that turn gong into Wu are pictographs of the long sleeves of the dancers' costumes.

'Shaman' *"Wu: The work of witches; magic, incantations. Two witches who dance to obtain rain."* Dr.L. Wieger, S.J

DANCING WU

The dancing Wu are associated with the great oneness and the healing arts that utilised Qi. The mobilisation of Qi through dancing became an ancient ritualistic custom for connecting to spirit and embodying unseen spirit. Shamans danced as part of their healing rituals, as if the movement was an expression of Qi flow itself. The notion of embodying spirit and surrendering to spirit, allowing it to express itself, was synonymous with being the Wu. Thus, as the shamans danced, they became the representatives of Great Spirit itself.

The next character to look at is 'Kou'.

KOU 'OPENING'

Kou is a pictograph depicting an entrance or opening. Some people have described these three openings as open mouths, praying or singing. This refers to the incantations and invocations used to bring spirit to earth as part of healing and manifestation ceremonies. They have also been referred to as the open mouths through which we are nourished. This is particularly interesting when we look at the final pictogram.

In the I Ching, Kou means 'Encountering'. It refers to the meeting of [Qian] The Heaven and [Xun] The Gentle Wind.

It states,

"When heaven and earth come to meet each other, all creatures prosper. It is necessary for elements, predestined to be joined and mutually dependent, to come to meet one another halfway. But the coming together must be free of dishonest ulterior motives, otherwise harm will result."

There are three openings or three mouths, which again refers to the three realms of heaven, earth and humankind. So the three openings could refer to the virtue required to connect ourselves as the bridge between Heaven and Earth. In the I Ching it states that, to connect with the heavens, one has to be in accord with the power and virtue of the way [Dao]. It could also mean three prayers, incantations or sets.

The final character to look at from the pictograph of Ling Chi and Reiki is 'Ling or Rei'.

LING OR REI 'SPIRIT'

One of the earliest concerns in ancient cultures was the water for growing crops. The water upon which they relied came in the form of rainfall. Without rain, they would have nothing to eat and drink. The final pictograph, Ling, shows rain falling out of clouds in the heavens. The horizontal line at the top symbolises Heaven. Below that is the character for cover, suggesting clouds. The vertical lines on the left and the right indicate the boundary of the clouds. There are four raindrops falling and the vertical line in the middle represents the downward motion of the raindrops.

Rainmaking was the role of the 'Wu' shaman using dance, invocation, prayer and ritual to contact Great Spirit and call upon the elements to create rain. According to Taoist tradition, the ruler of the manifest universe is a deity figure well known in Chinese popular culture called the Jade Emperor. He is said to be the Great Heavenly Emperor who sends Qi, the Heavenly Breath, streaming down, connecting Heaven and Earth and infusing mankind with vitality. It is no wonder then that inspired Wu shamans would serve crystal jade to the heavens in their rituals. In an ancient script [the great seal script] there is a pictograph showing the Jade being offered by the Wu.

WU OFFERING JADE

THE WHOLE PICTOGRAPH OF REIKI

The literal translation of this Pictograph tells the story of Wu shamans performing dance rituals to call upon the heavens to bless their communities with the rain for their crops. It is worth remembering that in those times, with the lack of light polluting the night sky, a greater affinity would have been possible with the cosmos. It must have been difficult not to feel a deep intimate connection to the universe when staring at the night sky from the planet's surface 3000 years ago.

So how do we go from rain to Spirit?

A more psycho-spiritual understanding of Ling tells us that, just like abundant rain falls out of the gathering clouds in heaven, so too does universal life force. Out of the Tai Yi, *[the primordial unity of Yin and Yang]*, the Dao *[Primordial Essence]*, the Yuang Qi *[Original Ki]* flows the Ling Chi *[The Soul Chi]*. It flows not out of the clouds but out of the void and descends in abundance, like the rains from heaven, as love and light.

The pictograph for Ling Chi and Reiki, tells the story of the shaman who invoked the supernatural power from Spirit to fall out of the void like rain. Being the Wu, the empty vessel, allows us to become the embodiment of that supernatural power, surrendering to it and in doing so, becoming the bridge between heaven and earth. When we stand tall, and recognise ourselves as the Wu, we are nourished by the Qi of heaven and earth, and just like rice nourishes us, our mind, body and spirits are nourished.

Reiki, then, is a practice that cultivates Ki by allowing us to become empty and surrender to the supernatural transcendent power of spirit, knowing oneself as inseparable from the cosmos. Becoming the loving servant rather than the controlling master requires us to surrender to and be informed by the subtle language that speaks through Ki. It is a language that we will struggle to hear if we are too full of noise. Slowly, through the practices we learn in Reiki, we become increasingly sensitive to the inner voice that steers us and guides us both in life and in treatment.

We must remember that Reiki existed in the hearts and minds of our ancestors. When viewed as an evolution of psycho-spiritual practices, we can begin to unbind Reiki and breathe fresh insight into its utilisation. Reiki revealed itself to Usui Sensei. He became a rainmaker. He discovered how to connect to Reiki and became an embodiment of the primordial essence. His legacy, the Usui Reiki Ryoho is the treasure map he left behind to enable others to do the same. Our journey is to tap into the rhythms of the universe, to see ourself as an expression of the cosmos, intimately connected at all times. It teaches us to invoke our own shamanic nature; sing and dance if we like and call upon the heavens to participate in our lives at every moment. To gather the life force, embody it and recognise it in others. To cultivate well- being, heal and restore our connection to the Heavens and the Earth. Our journey is to become a rainmaker.

YIN AND YANG

"Your soul isn't in your body, your body is in your soul."

Alan Watts.

In the Dao De Jing the concept of a primordial essence from which everything creatively unfolds is summed up in the following numerical accumulation.

$$0 - 1 - 2 - 3 - 10,000$$

Wuji   Taiji   Yin Yang

THE ZERO

Beginning with Wuji

The Primordial emptiness, the formless void.

THE ONE

The Primordial emptiness becomes the Primordial Unity

giving birth to Oneness Taiji.

THE TWO

The Primordial Unity becomes the two, heaven and earth

giving birth to Yang and Yin.

THE THREE

Yang and Yin through their eternal interplay

give birth to Qi.

THE TEN THOUSAND

From Qi all things are created

giving birth to the Ten Thousand Things.

So the emptiness of the void, gives birth to the great ocean of all existence, Primordial Unity, This oneness becomes the heavens [Yang] and the earth [Yin]. Qi is the substance that arises from the relationship between them. The symbol for Yin and Yang represents this interplay. Long before the symbol for Yin and Yang was established in its more recent guise, it was characterised in Chinese mythology by the Tiger [Yin] and the Dragon [Yang].

Tiger represented the earth and Dragon represented the spirit. Neither was able to conquer the other and so they signified the endless dance of opposing energies, coming together as eternal companions. The creative energies produced by them in their eternal battle with one another, spawning the ten thousand things.

DRAGON AND TIGER

Even though Yin and Yang operate in opposition to each other, one could not exist without the other. They are not polarised in a good versus evil way, because the loss of either pole would mean the disappearance of everything. For example, an electrical current has a positive and negative pole but the disappearance of either polarity would mean the disappearance of the current itself.

The polarity of heaven and earth are expressed as Yang [positive] and Yin [negative] and are often described as the sunny and shady sides of a mountain. Sit too long in the sun and you will need to seek the cool of the shade to balance your temperature. The art of life is not to seek Yang over Yin but to keep the two in balance because there cannot be one without the other. Balance, then, is found in the interplay of opposites, the masculine and feminine, the light and the dark, the rising and falling and the heavens and the earth.

As humans, we stand at the meeting point between the polarities of heaven and earth and, just like an electrical current, both polarities express themselves through us. The disappearance of either polarity would mean we would cease to exist. It is therefore a precarious situation that we find ourselves in when many of the earth's population are so involved in their day-to-day dramas that they forget they are part of nature and neglect to look up into the stars. Disregarding our natural environment disconnects us from our essential nature and closes our hearts. A closed heart is cut off from the vital essence of being and that ultimately leads to self-alienation, fear and suffering.

It is important for us to remember to maintain the balance between our earthbound nature and our spiritual nature. It is not by chance that, regardless of which subtle anatomy model you look at, energetically the meeting place between the realm of heaven and earth is the heart. Reiki has long promoted itself as helping to balance and generate emotional, mental and spiritual well-being. When we realise Ki as being the essential ingredient in the creative expression of existence we can see why.

I often hear people talking about Reiki as something they do, energy they channel from outside of themselves. Hawayo Takata spoke of Reiki as, *"A universal force from the Great Divine Spirit"* and as a *"Cosmic energy"*. But she also wrote of Reiki being; *"An Energy within oneself"*. After years of practicing Reiki, I have come to realise myself as part of its flow, connected to it and an expression of it. At first I recognised that I was a rainmaker and could call upon the universe to participate in my life. The flow though, didn't materialise from outside of me; instead it appeared to expand out of me from somewhere deep within. The more I opened, the more it flowed. I started to become mindful that where I stood on the Earth, the Heavens surrounded me in every direction and the medium for expression was myself! Just like a sprouting seed grows in both directions, I was both rooted to the earth and reaching out to the heavens. Slowly, I comprehended the inescapable truth, I was the universe and the universe was me.

In the Reiki pictograph we have seen that our journey is to stand between heaven and earth and, just like a tree, remain firmly rooted to the earth as we reach up towards the heavens. It would not be wrong to see ourselves as the latest fruition in the eternal interplay between Yin and Yang energies, for it is consciousness itself that is undergoing the greatest evolution in our time. The eternal quest of our ancestors for longevity has contributed to our knowledge and the very essence that flowed through them flows through us now. Though our bodies that we inhabit are but a season's leaves that will one day fall from the tree, we are also the essence that has flowed through every tree throughout all of time.

THE THREE REALMS

SANJIE

"Without awareness of bodily feeling and attitude, a person becomes split into a disembodied spirit and a disenchanted body."

Alexander Lowen

At the very roots of Taoist thinking is the concept of three realms, Heaven, Earth and Man existing as an expression of primordial unity.

The model of man standing upright between the heavens above and the earth below explains our place in the great scheme of things. The ancient 'rainmakers' danced between heaven and earth to invoke the benevolent spirits for rituals. The Wu shaman made offerings to the heavens in their rituals to draw upon the universal forces. In particular 'Crystal Jade' was offered because it was regarded as 'the very essence of heaven' and was compared to the virtues of life itself. In Japanese there is a kanji character 'Tama' that means 'jewel'. Tama is the character representing the connection between Heaven (一) and Earth (土). The stroke on the bottom right of Tama implies 'heaven's essence on earth'.

TAMA

I mentioned in Chapter 2 the popular animation series called Dragon Ball where the main character Goku learns Genki Dama, the method of gathering energy from the environment to create sphere's of Ki power called, spirit bombs. Goku gathers the Genki [Yuanqi], Original Ki, from the earth and heavens by standing with his arms reaching outstretched towards the sky, absorbing white particles of light into the Hara [belly] of his body. He then directs the energy to his right hand condensing it to form a ball of Ki. This is an example of how ancient philosophies have migrated and evolved throughout time and modern contemporary culture often draws upon these philosophies and relates to them remarkably accurately. The stance Goku uses is found in Qigong practices as an Earth and Heaven connection. The way of Tao suggests that the secret to prolonging a human being's life is to absorb the essence of 'Tian' meaning Heaven and 'Di' meaning Earth.

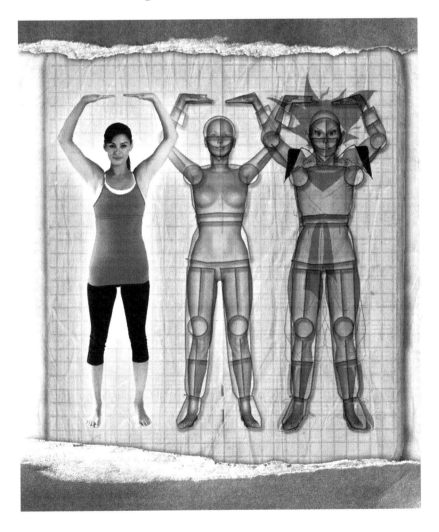

HEAVEN EARTH

So what separates Reiki from other Ki disciplines that have evolved up to the rediscovery of Reiki by Mikao Usui? The gathering of Qi in Taoist and Qigong practices had the ultimate goal of union with the great primordial oneness. Therefore great emphasis was placed on developing and refining energy through the various energy centres, 'Dantians', in the body to arrive at a point of reconnection to the cosmos. Chakra theory follows a similar concept of refining the self and ascending through the energy centres, developing self-awareness of our essential nature and awakening our divine consciousness in the crown Chakra.

I think it is easy to misunderstand these concepts and focus on developing the higher centres at the expense of the lower ones in an effort to acquire intuitive gifts. This is typical of a western attitude, where Spirituality is often approached from an intellectual rather than an experiential point of reference. As a result, people can often be left feeling disembodied and without a foundation on which to build their spiritual practice. Unfortunately, one of the great attractions to Reiki can also be its Achilles heel. Students are not required to develop a mindful awareness of their body before attaining Reiki, because, by its very nature, they are given it. Alas, unless guided by a good teacher we can end up with many top-heavy, ungrounded practitioners.

In Qigong, the approach is that energy must be gathered and refined before reconnection to universal oneness can occur. In Reiki it is the opposite, connection is made to the oneness and then refinement takes place, the practice comes after receiving it, not before. Because of this, practitioners can sometimes forget their foundations and lose sight of the importance of balancing the energies of heaven and earth.

What sets Reiki apart from everything else is that we are connected to the Reiki phenomenon by an initiation. Once the initiation has been received however, Reiki is similar to other practices in as much as it is about letting go of what stands in the way, becoming as empty as possible and allowing Reiki to flow through us to enrich our lives. A practitioner must seek to ground Reiki, cultivate that connection, integrate it and through daily practice surrender to it, allowing it to flow through them.

It would be wise for Reiki practitioners to develop awareness of the belly area before attempting anything else. This helps with our orientation and ensures we have a grounded practice. It supports the idea that we are part of the process and the energy that we manifest is something that flows from within us rather than thinking we have to go out there to find it. The Hara, and in particular the 'Seika Tanden', an energetic point three-finger widths below the belly button in the core of our belly, provides a point on which we as practitioners can focus our attention. Hawayo Takata referred to the Seika Tanden point herself when she wrote in her diary; "It lies in the bottom of your stomach about 2 inches below the navel" and how we must "let the energy come out from within."

By bringing our awareness to our Hara, we naturally bring ourselves into the present moment and remain firmly grounded. This enables us to take our position between heaven and earth and allows us to notice internal energy flow and become an empty vessel for Ki to naturally express itself through.

I am of the opinion that practicing both Reiki and Qigong has a direct and positive effect on the other. Many people who practice Qigong, including myself, will testify that it enhances our relationship to Reiki and helps to cultivate an awareness of energy. Most important of all, it reminds us of our role as a meeting point between the Earth and the Heavens through which Ki can emanate.

BECOMING THE EMPTY VESSEL - WU

"The journey of a thousand miles starts under your feet"

Dao De Jing

In Chinese philosophy, Qi comes from the emptiness, the formless void known as Wu. It is understood that through the study of our own formlessness we are able to experience the flow of Qi through us. This connection opens us up and informs what areas are causing restriction and require letting go. These can be caused by emotional trauma held deep within the body, experienced as muscular tension, restricted movement and pain. They can present themselves as phobias, allergies and diseases. They can create patterns of negative thinking and lead to destructive lifestyle choices. Sometimes they are not expressed beyond simple tensions. The less restriction there is, the greater the flow. To become empty, to unwind and release patterns in the body, we have to allow space for movement and change and let Reiki reawaken wholeness.

As we stand between the polarities of heaven and earth, we are the point at which the Yin of earth and the Yang of heaven converge. At first we realise our connection to them and, as we develop our relationship to these two polarities, we find ourselves to be a manifestation of them. The emptier we become, the greater the expression, until we arrive at a very simple truth, we are not living life, we are life.

This realisation awakens wholeness within us and our inner development becomes an act of letting go of all that isn't whole. Just like a sculptor carves away at a rock and reveals what he has always seen hidden within it. This is our task, to become like empty bamboo so that we reconnect to the essential flow of life through us. Once we awaken wholeness in ourselves we can observe what obstructs wholeness in others.

I attended a Richard Moss lecture in London's Russell Square one chilly November in 2005, and he came in carrying a jam jar filled with mud and water. He gave it a shake and then placed it on the table telling us he brought it from home especially to show us that we were like the water in the jar, cloudy and mixed up. He proceeded to talk about the importance of bringing the mind home to settle into the now. It was a fascinating presentation and the hours swept by. At the end, he returned to the jam jar on the table. The water was now completely clear and he said all you need for things to become crystal clear is to be still. It reminded me that the only place in a constantly changing and expanding universe where I can find stillness is within me and it is always there for me to visit if I choose to do so.

In Qigong there is a physical stance called the Wuji. This is the standing posture from which all movement arises. Wuji has been likened to empty bamboo because, before any forms are learnt, first we learn to stand as emptiness. We could call it the shaman's stance. Wuji means 'the formless void' or 'the beginning'. It relates to the infinite possibilities before the creation of Yin and Yang. As a stance it informs us of what is misaligned and out of balance that prevents wholeness within our being.

Through the Wuji we learn to root ourselves, take our place on the ground and stand tall. We learn where to focus our centre of gravity and become mindful of what is obstructing flow within. Most importantly of all, we learn to view earth as a living entity that we have grown out from. We exchange energy with the earth, we can give her what we no longer wish to carry and she will happily compost and recycle it into something more useful. Through the Wuji we can experience the integration of Yin and Yang energies in the body and begin to notice the focal point for these energies at the Lower Dantian [Seika Tanden in the Hara]. This is the reservoir into which Reiki can be gathered as part of our daily preparation. This practice helps us become mindful of what prevents flow and informs us how our actions can become more aligned to flow.

A client of mine who came to see me had been struggling with the fear of heights most of his life and in particular on exposed moving escalators. He had been to many therapists before me and had no success. We established this phobia went back to an operation performed on his feet when he was a teenager to correct claw foot. He had to relearn to walk after the operation and never really found his footing. As part of our sessions, I decided to teach him Wuji. After explaining the philosophy behind it and the posture and skeletal balance that was necessary I asked him where his centre of gravity was and he really didn't know. I observed that he seemed to spend a lot of time over-analysing and thinking about things and his energy was very high up around his head. With regard to his phobia he had been analysing it for years and so I made him aware of it. I then suggested he could bring his centre of gravity down from his head to his belly and I placed my hands either side of his abdomen to support him and show him the part of his body I wished him to experience. The Reiki naturally flowed through my hands into his abdomen and after just a few moments he opened his eyes in amazement. "That is the first time I have had the sensation of being in my body since I was 14 years old", he said. As I continued to guide him through the Wuji his breathing changed, becoming deeper and more relaxed, the tremors that he experienced in his arms and legs subsided and for the first time he found himself planted and rooted into the earth.

Part of the operation he had when he was 14 years old involved lifting his toes and fusing them to the foot. This resulted in his toes never actually touching the ground and psychologically had led him to feel very unstable. So I emphasised the importance of distributing his weight through the soles of his feet and finding balance between two points at the front of his feet and his heel. As a result, he realised he no longer required his toes to be balanced when standing and this gave him a huge amount of confidence. I then asked him to walk around the room to experience motion and he continued to be amazed by the sensation of his feet and the contact with the earth. He e-mailed me the following day to say that he had gone to the shopping centre and had managed to walk up an exposed escalator unaided without any fear in his body at all. As evidence of its efficacy, it was a fantastic exercise into the benefits of this simple standing posture.

I am including the Wuji exercise in this book purely because it informs us of the flow within our own system and reveals where our body requires unwinding and is holding contraction. As Reiki is a self-healing and development system, the Wuji can be an incredibly useful exercise to import from Qigong. I have seen enough Reiki practitioners standing on one leg and bent over a healing table with terrible postures to know this exercise will benefit many. Remember, if you are comfortable and standing with good upright posture and your centre of gravity is nice and low, you will be a clear-grounded channel through which Reiki can flow.

EXERCISE FOR WUJI STANDING ON THE EARTH

Place your feet approximately shoulder width apart, heels and toes parallel. Imagine yourself in the saddle of a horse and allow your knees to flex gently

Begin rocking forwards and backwards from your heel to your toes whilst maintaining full contact with the earth through the soles of your feet. This will activate the yong quan [bubbling spring] points in your feet. As you continue to rock gently, allow the hips and pelvis to become fluid and part of the movement.

After a few minutes, allow the rocking to slowly reduce, winding you in, finding the perfect point of balance and stillness.

Allow yourself to become aware of your breath and gently bring your breath deeper down inside your body to your belly.

As you begin to feel what you notice inside that requires unwinding, make minute adjustments to your posture so that your skeletal system is supporting you and your muscles can relax as much as possible.

Become aware of your spine and allow it to extend as it feels supported by the foundations of feet, legs, hips and pelvis below.

When you feel a synergy between, breath, balance and stillness, allow your arms to rise up from your sides and direct your palms into your lower abdomen as if you are a pregnant mother cradling your tummy.

Breathe, relax and feel the connection between the earth below you, the heavens above, your breath anchoring you to the now and your hands radiating Ki into your belly. Enjoy

WUJI

THE THREE MODELS OF KI FLOW

Understanding the complexity of the energetic structure through which Ki flows has occupied philosophers for centuries and I could write another complete book on it. I am reluctant to stray too far from the very simple idea that we are a vessel through which energy can stream from the Heaven and Earth for it distracts us a little from the idea of flow.

For our purposes here, I will give a modest overview of the three principle subtle anatomy models that have evolved, to make sense of Ki flow without going too deeply into them. These three models are, the Dantian theory from China, the Chakra system from the Vedic cultures and The Hara system from Japan.

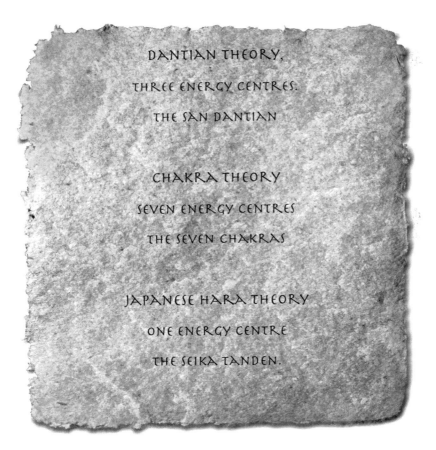

DANTIAN THEORY,

THREE ENERGY CENTRES.

THE SAN DANTIAN

CHAKRA THEORY

SEVEN ENERGY CENTRES

THE SEVEN CHAKRAS

JAPANESE HARA THEORY

ONE ENERGY CENTRE

THE SEIKA TANDEN.

SAN DANTIAN

THE THREE DANTIAN

SAN DANTIAN

The Chinese believe that the human microcosm [cosmos in miniature] is a mirror of the greater macrocosm made up of the heavens, the earth and man. The relationship between these inner and outer realms gives an insight into their philosophy, that all components of the universe are intimately related. The Dantian model and the Chakra model share a rudimentary principle that is consistent through each of them. Humankind stands between two energy sources, the heavens and the earth. Energy is gathered from them and is distributed throughout the physical body via subtle channels.

Within the human microcosm there is an orbit known as the microcosmic orbit through which the Yin and Yang energies that flow from the external polarities of heaven and earth are brought into balance. In just the same way as a tree has roots to connect deeply to the earth for stability, and requires branches to reach to the sky for nourishment, so do we. Imagine, if you will, an opening through the top of your head up into the vast expanse of heaven drawing heaven-energy downward into your body. Then through the soles of your feet earth-energy being gathered upwards, just like sap being drawn through the roots of a tree. The microcosmic orbit has points to connect to the flow of Yin and Yang and our human body then becomes the "meeting-place of heaven and earth. The essential points that access the polarities of Yang and Yin are as follows;

THE YONGQUAN - BUBBLING SPRING

IN THE SOULS OF THE FEET.

THE BAIHUI - HUNDRED CONVERGENCES

AT THE TOP OF THE HEAD.

THE LAOGONG - HOUSE OF LABOUR

IN THE PALMS OF EACH HAND.

Laogong   Yongquan   Baihui

MASSAGE OF HEAVEN AND EARTH POINTS EXERCISE

It can be helpful to stimulate the heaven and earth points in the soles of your feet and the top of your head to improve your connection to heaven and earth. To work on the yong quan point in the soles of your feet, sit in a straight-backed chair (or on the floor) and rest the ankle of your left leg over the thigh of the right leg. Cradle your left foot between the palms of your left and right hands, ensuring your fingers are aligned towards the toes. This connects Yong Quan with the Lao Gong in the palms of your hands. Allow Reiki to flow for a few minutes and then, using your right thumb, massage the yong quan point gently. Continue for 2-3 minutes, and then switch sides. When you have finished, relax and notice the movement of energy up your legs feeling the connection with your pelvic floor.

To stimulate the Baihui point at the top of your head, grip your cranium either side fingers pointing to the back gently pressed into the cranium floor at the medulla oblongata. Work your way up through the centre of your cranium over the top of your head to the middle of the forehead. Repeat as necessary.

The microcosmic orbit has three reservoirs known as Dantians [fields of elixir]. The three Dantian [San Dantian] reflect the three realms [Sanjie]. The Upper Dantian is conveniently related to the heavens [formlessness] the Lower Dantian related to the earth [desire] and the Middle Dantian to the expression of the meeting of the two polarities [form]. The Upper Dantian is located behind the forehead similar to the Ajna Chakra [3rd eye]. The Lower Dantian is located inside the body 2 inches below the naval] just above the Svadhistana Chakra and the Middle Dantian is located in the chest at the Anahata Chakra.

In Japan these three reservoirs have been imported by some traditions and are referred to as follows;

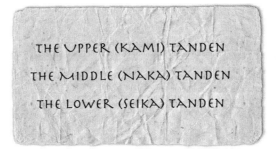

THE UPPER (KAMI) TANDEN

THE MIDDLE (NAKA) TANDEN

THE LOWER (SEIKA) TANDEN

Two super highways connect the Dantian's reservoirs vertically through the front and rear midlines. These two superhighways join to form one complete circle of energetic current when the tip of the tongue touches the upper palate in the mouth and the Hui Yin point at the perineum is squeezed and form the microcosmic orbit. A third channel, the Chong Mai [Thrusting Channel], runs vertically through the centre of the body, connecting the perineum and the crown. The Chong Mai closely corresponds to the Sushumna Channel in the Chakra system. There are a further five main channels which, together, make up the eight extraordinary meridians which represent the bodies deepest level of energetic structure. Together these channels circulate Qi around the system from the Dantian reservoirs.

An analogy that helps us to understand this system is that of an ancient irrigation network of reservoirs and canals that distributed water for farming. The Dantian are like these reservoirs, storing Qi to ensure it is plentiful. The meridians like the canals distributing Qi through its network to where it is needed and our body's vital systems, like the trees and plants, being nourished. This system helped farmers to balance the elements and survive the droughts. As long as the reservoirs were replenished by rainfall, there was always a supply of water to the crops.

THE THREE TREASURES

SAN BAO

"Everyone and everything in Heaven, Mother Earth and countless planets, stars, galaxies and universes is vibration, which is the field of Jing Qi Shen".

Zing Gang Sha

There are three types of essence expressed through the Dantian system that reflect the outer cosmos known as the three treasures. [San Bao]; Jing, Qi and Shen. They are the basic elements of life and cannot be separated. They are intimately linked and supplement one another, merging to form a unity; 'The internal elixir', which is sometimes also referred to as the 'Golden Elixir'. It is through the gathering, nourishment and refinement of these Three Treasures that Taoists advanced their studies. It was understood; the inner development and refinement of each elixir took them energetically towards the ultimate goal of consciously reuniting once again with the cosmos.

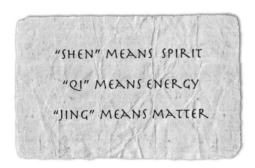

"SHEN" MEANS SPIRIT

"QI" MEANS ENERGY

"JING" MEANS MATTER

In the book Soul Healing Miracles by Zing Gang Sha, the author states,

"The Source field carries the Jing Qi Shen of the Source that can remove soul, mind, body blockages of sickness and transform the Jing Qi Shen of a human being's spiritual, mental, emotional and physical bodies from head to toe, skin to bone, to restore them to health."

IN THE UPPER DANTIAN

WE FIND SHEN

IN THE MIDDLE DANTIAN

WE FIND QI

IN THE LOWER DANTIAN

WE FIND JING

It is believed that the Three Treasures, are the fundamental building blocks for all facets of life. They are stored in the Dantian and distributed around the body via meridians

SHEN - is heavenly, the subtle energy of spirit and the most Yang form of Qi. It is a form of cosmic consciousness. The reservoir for Shen is the Upper Dantian. Shen is said to escape through the eyes, which is why meditation is regarded as a powerful way to contain it. Shen is reflected in the clarity and luminosity of the eyes and in the focus, lucidity and intensity of the intellectual and emotional process.

QI - is the balance point. It is the vital life force of existence and is formed through the interplay of Yin and Yang, [water and fire] it is the inner alchemy that produces the steam like vapour of Qi. The reservoir for Qi is in the Middle Dantian. Qi is gathered and refined through the breath in 'the house of breath'.

JING - is pre-natal qi from parents. It is the material basis for life, which can be transmuted and transformed into a new and separate individual life through procreation. It is our capacity to conserve and preserve the essence that determines our health, vitality and lifespan. The reservoir for Jing is the lower elixir field, the lower Dantian. Gathering energy into the lower Dantian provides nourishment and serves to raise Jing up the Du Mai [governing vessel].

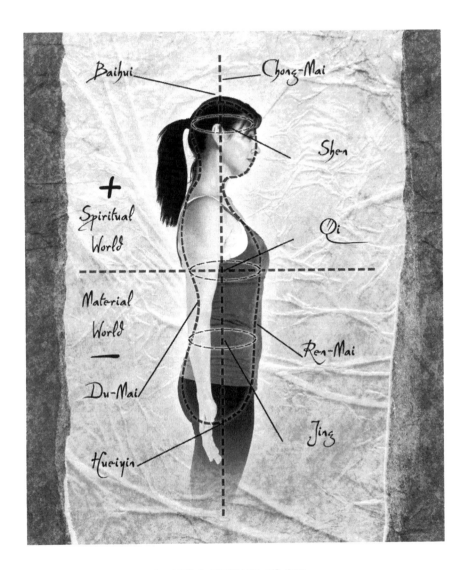

MICRO COSMIC ORBIT

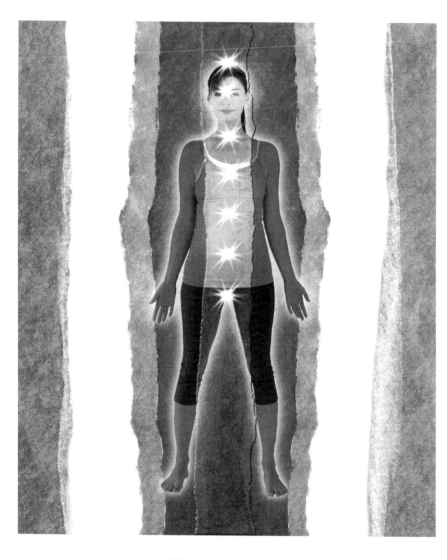

SEVEN CHAKRAS

THE SEVEN CHAKRAS

"Emotions are energy in motion. To Deny emotion
is to deny the vital energy of our life"

John Bradshaw

In some quarters Chakra theory has been dismissed as a new age addition to Reiki, insisting that they were never part of the original system. Reiki researcher James Deacon suggests.

"The whole concept of Chakras is really alien to Japanese healing practices (one – or more – of Takata Sensei's students, it seems, introduced the Chakra system into Reiki probably in the late 70's as a frame of reference for New-Age oriented westerners)".

One of those students who advocated the use of Chakras to understand the theory of the human energy system was John Harvey Gray, who, till his death on 12th January 2011, was the oldest surviving student of Hawayo Takata. He developed his theory of emotionality and the Chakras and asserted that the musculature, not the Chakras, hold emotions. He said "When they are not fully expressed, emotions can get locked in the body creating a state of muscular tension which prevents energy flow through the Chakras".

I am personally a great advocate of Chakra theory, I even wrote a book on it. When giving Reiki, an understanding of the aspects of each Chakra can be of great value, as patterns of emotional or psychological behaviour are assigned to particular Chakras. As a model to aid understanding of the relationship between energy restrictions and psychological and emotional impacts it is possibly the clearest and easiest model to comprehend.

The Chakra system, like the Dantian system, is a model that reflects our connection between earth and heaven. This is achieved through a central energy channel known as Sushumna, which runs through the Canalis Centralis, a hollow region in the spine. Two further channels, called Ida and Pingala, spiral upwards in a dance of opposing duality [Yin and Yang] from the perineum, intersecting along the length of this vertical channel. There is also a network of finer channels known as Nadis that interconnect these three channels. When twenty-one Nadis intersect, a major Chakra is formed. There are 7 major Chakras in total. Starting at the perineum. The Sushumna channel runs vertically up from the Base Chakra to the Crown Chakra and these two Chakras open up at each end to form our connection to both earth and spirit. Five further Chakras are distributed along the length of the vertical channel where Ida and Pingala meet.

IDA AND PINGALA

These three main distribution channels carry the energy between the Chakras, which is then further circulated through the finer Nadis channels. These can be likened to the meridians from Dantian theory, which carry vital energy through the system. It is believed that when there is a disturbance to the flow of universal life force energy along any of these pathways, it causes an imbalance leading to a physical ailment or disease. The Chakra system accurately overlays onto the endocrine system, which is believed to be the vehicle that steps down vital energy for use in the physical body.

It is thought that as our consciousness evolves, the concentration of Ki moves up from the Root Chakra through each of the Chakras in turn, becoming higher in vibration as it moves up. The physical, emotional and psychological aspects assigned to each Chakra represent a journey. As we progress through life and integrate various experiences, we develop our understanding and potentiality, awakening our divine consciousness in the crown Chakra.

For those wanting a more comprehensive description of the Chakra system, read my previous book, Reiki And The Seven Chakras.

MEDITATION ON THE SEVEN CHAKRAS

CROWN CHAKRA - Once you are completely relaxed, bring your awareness to the area above your crown and concentrate fully on that area. Pay attention to what you notice and be curious about the sensations you feel above your head. Begin to visualise a thousand beautiful white flower petals opening from buds to full flowers. Just see thousands opening one after another.

THIRD EYE - Bring your awareness down into your head at the height of your forehead and notice how it feels. Begin to imagine a triangular window to your mind and through it bright light shining in, cleansing and clearing your mind, purifying your mind.

THROAT - Now bring your awareness down to your throat, notice the sensations in that area of your body. Be aware of how free or restricted this area feels. Begin to imagine the vibration of sound in this area, the type of vibration that you can feel and causes your body to resonate. Notice the feeling of that visualisation in this part of your body.

HEART - Bring your awareness down to your chest area. Feel your breath and compare the in breath with the out breath. Be aware of any sensations and feelings in this area. Begin to imagine a strong breeze blowing through your chest, feel it moving through you, clearing things away as it blows through you.

SOLAR PLEXUS - Now bring your awareness down to your diaphragm area. Notice what you are feeling and experiencing here. What you need to release and let go of. Begin to visualise burning coals or logs on a fire. Imagine stoking the fire and seeing the flames dancing before you.

SACRAL - Bring your awareness down further now to your pelvis area. Once again, assess what you notice about this part of your body. Begin to imagine here the surface of a beautiful lake.

BASE - Finally, bring your awareness down to your perineum at the base of your spine. Focus all of your attention on this area and notice what you feel here. Imagine the soil of the earth as dark brown and roots growing down under the earth.

THE HARA

THE HARA

"Empty the heart, fill the abdomen."

Laozi

There is some confusion between the hara system found in Japan and the Dantian System from China. Many people think they are one and the same but the Hara System, by virtue of its location in the belly, only encompasses one energy point, the Seika Tanden. This is in the same location of the Lower Dantian from the Chinese model. The other energy centres from the Dantian system are not generally referred to in the Japanese Hara system as they exist outside of the belly region. In the Hara system it is the mind itself that is concentrated into the Seika Tanden and all energy rather than being circulated, emanates from here.

It is believed the vital life force of an individual, is said to reside in the hara. In Japan a famous way to commit suicide is to commit Hara – Kiri [cut the Hara]. A more classic Samurai word for this type of suicide is 'Seppuku' which Reiki Sensei, Chujiro Hayashi, famously committed in 1940 to end his life.

You cannot be conscious of the hara without dropping into the NOW which is why fulfillment is said to arise out of sinking the mind into the hara. Once the mind is focused here, all movement and expression comes from a place of grounded mindfulness. Individual understanding of this energetic space through breathing meditations naturally brings us into balance by focusing our mind on the present moment. The arising benefits of this meditation allow for a growing awareness of our true nature. It provides knowledge of the foundation within our body from which energy can emanate. As a practitioner develops their awareness of themselves as a point of expression between heaven and earth the result is energy flow. Through the steps offered to use the breath to ground awareness of their mind into the hara, a practitioner is brought into a deeper sense of the now. Once this is mastered an embodied state of mind is achieved and the intention for Reiki to be transmitted is all that is required to create flow.

MEDITATION ON SEIKA TANDEN

Assume either the seiza posture, [sitting on your heels]
cross-legged or on a chair.

Place your hands comfortably in your lap

Place the tip of your tongue into the roof of your mouth
just behind your front teeth

Close your eyes and focus your awareness on your breathing

Notice the rise and fall of your belly as you breath

As you sink your awareness deeper into your belly
allow it to direct your breath

Notice the sensations of being breathed by your Hara

Allow your breathing to become deeply relaxed

Relax into your hara

Notice whatever sensations occur

When you feel its time to finish open your eyes

PART 2.

ONCE UPON A TIME ON

MOUNT KURAYAMA

THE MOUNTAIN AS THE MANDALA.

*"Great things are done when men and mountains meet.
This is not done by jostling in the street".*

William Blake

Mountains have always been places sought out for spiritual retreat and refuge, places to meditate and seek the spiritual realms. Due to their lofty elevation they offer a detached view, a higher perspective above the mundane world, taking us closer to the heavens. Mountains have been worshipped throughout history and are often steeped in superstitions. In Japan it is believed mountains are home to the Tengu, originally 'bird like beings' that slowly took on human form with long noses and wings. They are said to have magical powers and are seen as guardians of the shrines and temples.

There are also Kami called Ugajin that are often depicted with the body of a snake and the head of a man or woman. They appear in both masculine and feminine form and remind me of Ida and Pingala from the chakra system.

UGAJIN

Energetically, mountains are often places of significance where energy vortices connecting heaven and earth are found. In Japan, there are various sects that regard mountains as places of supernatural power. The Shugendo sect for example is a Japanese religion where the Shugenja [Priests] make pilgrimages into the sacred mountains to perform magic rituals to acquire supernatural and miraculous powers. Shugendo is a form of esoteric Buddhism with Shamanistic and Taoist influences and is based on mountain worship. In the book 'Tantric Buddhism in East Asia' by Richard K Payne he says;

"Shugendo is regarded as the Vajrayana in Japan. Vajrayana of shugendo (shugendo mikkyo) is a dharma teaching where the mountain is considered as the supernatural mandala."

It was Kobodaishi, a tantric master, who brought Vajrayana Buddhism to Japan in the early 9th century and went on to establish the Shingon school of Buddhism. The story is told that Kobodaishi had been heading for an illustrious career when he met a Buddhist Priest;

"A Buddhist priest showed me a text called the Mantra of Akashagarbha. Believing what the Great Sage [the Buddha] says of the truth, I hoped for a result, as if rubbing pieces of wood together to make fire. I climbed Mount Otaki and meditated at Cape Muroto. The valleys reverberated with the echo of my voice, and the Bright Star [Venus] appeared in the sky. From that time on, I despised the fame and wealth of the court and city; I thought only about spending my life in the midst of the precipices and thickets of the mountains".

Central to Kobodaishi's philosophy was that initiation from a teacher formed a bridge between Dainichi Nyora [The Cosmic Buddha] and the student. The practice, sometimes known as the 'Diamond way', uses rituals, symbols and mantras as it seeks to eliminate duality. Vajrayana Buddhism is esoteric in the sense that the transmission of certain teachings only occurs directly from teacher to student during an initiation and cannot be simply learned from a book. In Tibetan Buddhism the Dalai Lama is the most well known Lama of Vajrayana.

Kobodaishi founded the Garan temple on Mount Koya [Koyasan], which went on to become the most hallowed centre of Shingon Buddhism with shrines to Dainichi Nyorai, the Cosmic Buddha, and Yakushi Nyorai, The Buddha of medicine and healing.

A little earlier, the first esoteric temple was placed on Mount Kurama by Tendai monks. Here there were shrines to Bishamonten, 'Protector of the North' and Amida Nyorai who is often seen accompanied by Senju Kannon, the Thousand-Armed Goddess of Compassion.

Much later, another Buddhist deity unique to Kurama was included. The Defender Lord, Maoson, who represents the power of Earth. The current leadership, the Kurama- kokyo sect says these three deities create a trinity called the "Sonten". They say;

"Bishamonten represents the Sun, Kannon represents love, and Maoson, represents power, together they make up the Spiritual Kings of the World".

Interestingly Maoson has a similar legend to ascended master Sanat Kamara, who is, according to the theosophical teachings of Alice Baily and C.W Leadbeater, Lord of Earth and humanity. It is believed he appears as a 16- year old boy with 'Peacock feathers' growing from his hind and came from the same bright star, [Venus] that Kobodaishi was entranced by.

The question is, do the complex factions represented in the mountains of Japan offer us any clues to the origins of Reiki? Could there possibly be a thread that ties all these various beliefs together that relates to our healing practice? A thread that only the innocence of childlike vision could naively attempt to unravel? Later in this book I will be discussing the Reiki symbology and asking why Mikao Usui chose to include them in the Reiki practice. I will be looking for the clues to a deeper story that may or may not make sense of it all. Before I do, I wish to share a transcript of the story of Reiki told by Hawayo Takata from an original voice recording.

MIKAO USUI

"This is the story of Dr. Mikao Usui who is the originator of the Usui Reiki Ryoho."

Hawayo Takata

Between 1945 and 1970, it is believed Mrs Takata was the only Reiki master active in the world. Takata Sensei was a Japanese American; born and raised in Hawaii to Japanese immigrants and very much Japanese in her thinking and life style. When reading the stories she told, we have to bear in mind several factors. Not only the times in which she lived and anti-Japanese sentiment after the war, but also the requirement to have Reiki accepted in a predominantly Christian culture. There are many who have sadly attempted to discredit her stories, but lets not forget, what she shared kept alive the legends of Chujiro Hayashi and Mikao Usui. We must also remember it is the essence within the storyteller's tales that speaks to our hearts.

It is worth noting that Hawayo Takata referred to the system of Reiki as both, 'The Usui Reiki Ryoho' and the 'Usui Shiki Ryoho', the latter being found on the certificates she issued. Until 1982, Reiki was passed on from teacher to student orally with no written notes or records of its history or teachings. Therefore, all information about Reiki at that time came to us through the spoken word of Mrs Takata. It is also important to remember what Takata Sensei said about the story she told; "This is how it was told to me". She had no reason to make up such a story, she was simply passing on the teachings in the tradition they had been passed to her by Chujiro Hayashi.

What follows are extracts from a word for word transcript of a tape recording made of Hawayo Takata in 1979 when she was 78 years old. She tells the story of the discoveries and motivations that steered Mikao Usui to meditate upon Mount Kurama, that led to his visionary experiences, that became the foundation of Reiki. This recording was made just a year and a half before her transition and is reproduced here with the permission of Elizabeth Latham. I have punctuated the extracts with my own thoughts as I go.

MIKAO USUI

"THIS IS THE STORY OF DR. MIKAO USUI WHO IS THE ORIGINATOR OF THE USUI REIKI RYOHO. THAT IS IN JAPANESE, WHICH MEANS THE USUI REIKI SYSTEM OF NATURAL HEALING.

IN THE BEGINNING OF THE STORY DR. USUI WAS THE PRINCIPAL OF THE DOSHISHA UNIVERSITY IN KYOTO. ALSO MINISTER ON SUNDAY, AND AT THE UNIVERSITY THEY HAD A CHAPEL. SO HE WAS A FULLY-FLEDGED CHRISTIAN MINISTER WHO GAVE BIBLE LESSONS ON SUNDAYS TO THE STUDENTS AND MY TEACHER WAS HAYASHI, WHO WAS HIS PUPIL AND ALSO HE CARRIED ON THE WORK AFTER DR. USUI'S PASSING. DR.CHUJIRO HAYASHI WAS HIS NUMBER 1 DISCIPLE AND IT IS THROUGH DR. HAYASHI THAT I HAVE LEARNED ABOUT DR. USUI. I HAVE NEVER MET HIM AND HE SAID THAT DR. USUI WAS A GENIUS, A VERY, VERY BRILLIANT, INTELLIGENT GREAT PHILOSOPHER, AND A GREAT SCHOLAR."

Hawayo Takata explains in the transcript that Mikao Usui, on being asked if he could heal like it was written in the bible, resigned from the Doshisha University and went in search of a method of physical healing. Some have claimed that, upon making inquiries about Mikao Usui to Doshisha University, that they had never heard of him. However, Reiki researcher Elizabeth Latham writes; *"He lost his faith for a period of time and left the Church and Doshisha. over a dispute. He was well known all over Japan and had thousands of followers from his belief in the Holy Spirit and that Christianity should be made Japanese, to suit the Japanese mind"*. Clearly more information will come to light on this subject in the future. We pick up the story in Kyoto.

TAKATA SAYS "AT THAT TIME, NARA WAS THE SEAT OF BUDDHISM BUT KYOTO HAD THE MOST PEOPLE AND THE BIGGEST MONASTERIES IN JAPAN. AND SO HE DECIDED TO VISIT EVERY SINGLE ONE. SO, HE STARTED WITH THE MOST BIGGEST TEMPLE, THE SHIN, AND WHEN HE ARRIVED THERE HE MET A MONK, AND HE SAID "DO THE SUTRAS SAY THAT BUDDHA HEALED, IS IT WRITTEN DOWN IN THE SUTRAS THAT BUDDHA HAD HEALED LEPROSY, TUBERCULOSIS, AND THE BLIND, BY LAYING ON OF HANDS?" AND THE MONK

ANSWERED, "YES, IT IS WRITTEN IN THE SUTRAS." [USUI] SAID, "HAVE YOU MASTERED THE ART? CAN YOU DO IT?" AND THE MONK SAID, "WELL, IN BUDDHISM, PHYSICAL IS VERY IMPORTANT, BUT WE MINISTER THE PEOPLE SO THEY HAVE BETTER MINDS. WE WANT TO STRAIGHTEN THEIR MINDS FIRST SO THEY'LL BECOME MORE SPIRITUAL AND THEN SHOW MORE GRATITUDE AND LEARN ALL, EVERYTHING OF LIFE AND WE MONKS DO NOT HAVE TIME FOR THE PHYSICAL IN REACHING THE SPIRITUAL GROWTH, SPIRITUAL HEALING IS FIRST." DR. USUI BOWED AND SAID, "THANK YOU". THEN HE WENT ALSO TO THE DIFFERENT TEMPLES AND EVERYONE HAD THE SAME ANSWER. THEY SAID, "YES, IT IS REGISTERED IN THE SUTRAS, AND THEREFORE WE ACCEPT AND BELIEVE THAT BUDDHA WAS A HEALER. BUT, WE ARE TRYING TO HEAL THE MIND FIRST, AND THEREFORE WE DO NOT KNOW ANYTHING ABOUT HEALING THE BODY." AFTER DAYS, DAYS, AND MONTHS OF SEARCH DR. USUI WAS VERY DEPRESSED. BUT HE DID NOT GIVE UP. HE SAID, "I HAVE ONE MORE PLACE TO GO".

FINALLY, HE LEARNED IT IN A ZEN TEMPLE. AND WHEN HE APPROACHED THE TEMPLE, HE RANG THE BELL, AND A LITTLE PAGEBOY CAME OUT. AND HE SAID, "I WOULD LIKE TO SPEAK TO THE HIGHEST MONK OF THIS GRAND TEMPLE". HE SAID, "PLEASE COME IN. AND WHO ARE YOU?" AND HE SAID, "I AM MIKAO USUI. AND I WOULD LIKE TO STUDY BUDDHISM, AND THEREFORE I WOULD LIKE TO MEET THE MONK." SO THE MESSAGE WAS DELIVERED, AND WHEN THE MONK CAME OUT, HE WAS ABOUT TWENTY THREE YEARS OLD MONK, WITH A LOVELY FACE, LIKE A CHILD, INNOCENT LOOKING, BEAUTIFUL FACE, KINDLY VOICE, AND VERY GENTLE. HE SAID, "COME IN. AND SO YOU ARE INTERESTED IN BUDDHISM." HE SAID "YES, BUT FIRST, I WOULD LIKE TO ASK YOU A QUESTION. DOES THE ZEN BELIEVE IN HEALING?" HE SAID, "YES, WE DO. IT IS WRITTEN IN THE SUTRAS THAT THE BUDDHA DID IT, AND SO IN BUDDHISM WE HAVE THE HEALING." "WELL, CAN YOU HEAL THE PHYSICAL SELF?" HE SAID, "NOT YET". AND SO HE SAID, "WHAT DO YOU MEAN BY NOT YET?" HE SAID, "OH, WE MONKS ARE VERY, VERY BUSY, GIVING AH DISCOURSES, LECTURES AND PREACHING SO THAT THE MIND CAN BE ATTUNED FOR THE SPIRITUAL LEVEL. AND WE WANT TO BETTER THE MIND BEFORE WE TOUCH THE PHYSICAL." "AND THEN HOW ARE YOU GOING TO GET THE PHYSICAL TRAINING?" HE SAID, "THAT WILL COME".

In this part of the story, Hawayo Takata emphasises, over and over again, the message that the monks gave to Mikao Usui. The mind requires purifying to attune it to spirit before the physical body can be healed.

"HE SAID, "I WOULD LIKE TO JOIN YOUR MONKS, YOUR PRIESTS AND THEN STUDY HERE". IT TOOK HIM ABOUT THREE YEARS TO GO THROUGH ALL THE SUTRAS IN THE TEMPLE. AND WHEN MEDITATION HOUR CAME, DR. USUI SAT WITH THE OTHER MONKS IN HOURS AND HOURS OF MEDITATION HE SAID, "THE JAPANESE CHARACTER THAT IS WRITTEN IN THE SUTRAS, ALL THESE CHARACTERS, ORIGINALLY THEY CAME FROM CHINA. WE HAVE ADOPTED THE CHINESE CHARACTERS AS JAPANESE CHARACTERS, AND SO WHEN YOU READ THE SUTRAS, YOU CANNOT UNDERSTAND, BUT IT IS JUST LIKE ENGLISH PEOPLE READING LATIN. YOU KNOW IT, BUT THE CHARACTERS ARE READ AS WRITTEN." SO FINALLY,

HE WENT DEEP INTO THE CHINESE CHARACTERS AND BECAME A MASTER OF THE CHINESE CHARACTERS. AND AFTER THAT WAS COMPLETED, HE SAID, "NOT ENOUGH". "AFTER ALL, BUDDHA WAS A HINDU, AND THEREFORE, "HE SAID, "I SHOULD STUDY THE SANSKRIT. AND IF I STUDY THE SANSKRIT, THERE MAY BE SOMETHING IN SANSKRIT, NOTES TAKEN BY THE BUDDHA'S DISCIPLES, BECAUSE BUDDHA HAD MANY, MANY DISCIPLES, AND THAT'S HOW THE SCRIPTURES WERE WRITTEN."

In this extract Hawayo Takata clearly states that what Mikao Usui studied had migrated from Hinduism into China and then onto Japan. This is the same route that many of the ancient spiritual concepts we have looked at took as they evolved across cultures.

"THEREFORE, WHEN HE WENT INTO STUDYING THE SANSKRIT, AND WHEN HE LATER STUDIED VERY HARD TO MASTER IT, HE FOUND A FORMULA. JUST AS PLAIN AS DAY. NOTHING HARD, BUT VERY SIMPLE. LIKE TWO AND TWO EQUALS FOUR, THREE AND THREE EQUALS SIX, AS SIMPLE AS THAT.

"AND SO HE SAID, "VERY WELL, I'VE FOUND IT. NOW, I HAVE TO TRY TO INTERPRET THIS, BECAUSE IT WAS WRITTEN 2500 YEARS AGO. BECAUSE I DO NOT KNOW IF THIS WILL WORK OR NOT. BUT I HAVE TO GO THROUGH THE TEST. AND GOING THROUGH THIS TEST," HE SAID, "I CANNOT GUARANTEE MYSELF WHETHER I WILL LIVE THROUGH IT, OR NOT. BUT IF I DON'T TRY THE TEST," HE SAID", EVERYTHING WILL BE LOST. WE'LL GO BACK THREE YEARS. HE TALKED IT OVER WITH THE MONK, AND THE MONK SAID, "YES, YOU ARE A VERY COURAGEOUS MAN. WHERE ARE YOU GOING TO TEST THIS, RIGHT IN THIS TEMPLE?"

HE SAID "NO. I WOULD LIKE TO GO UP INTO THE MOUNTAINS", AND HE WENT UP TO MOUNT KURAMA. AND HE SAID "I WILL TEST MYSELF FOR TWENTY ONE DAYS. AND IF I DO NOT COME BACK ON THE NIGHT OF THE TWENTY-FIRST DAY, ON THE TWENTY-SECOND DAY MORNING, SEND OUT A SEARCH PARTY INTO THE FOREST TO FIND MY BODY. I WILL BE DEAD." AND SO, WITH THAT FAREWELL, HE LEFT, AND HE SAID, "I SHALL GO THROUGH THIS MEDITATION WITHOUT FOOD, ONLY WATER.

SO HE PICKED UP THE WATER AND HE CLIMBED UP IN THE MOUNTAINS".

Here Hawayo Takata is stating that Mikao Usui found the secret to healing and the origins of Reiki in an ancient Sanskrit formula. It is important to remember at this stage that Hawayo Takata is relating the story told to her by Chujiro Hayashi. There are many ancient Sanskrit healing sutras that may have been his inspiration however to date, no one can say for certain if there was one in particular that formed the foundation of Reiki. It is likely his meditation retreat contained different practices and meditations and certainly we know 21-day retreats in the mountains were by no means the exclusive domain of Mikao Usui.

As discussed earlier, mountains are often regarded as mystical places. The Shugendo sect, for example, regards mountains as places of supernatural power and the Shugenja [Priests] make pilgrimages to the mountains to perform rituals at their power places. The Reiki pictograph tells the story of shamans and sorcerers who invoke the supernatural power of spirit from the void for their rituals. Are not Shugenja [Priests] then part of this ancient lineage of shamans and sorcerers? Their rituals part of an evolution of spiritual practices that have evolved and migrated through time? Regardless of whether Mikao Usui found a secret formula in an ancient Sanskrit sutra or not, the fact he felt compelled to retreat to Mount Kurama, echoes many spiritual traditions. Even Kobodaishi the founder of Shingon Buddhism abandoned his life in the capital and threw himself into the life of a mountain ascetic.

"HE FOUND A STREAM THAT WAS CLOSE TO WATER, THEREFORE HE SAT UNDER A BIG PINE TREE, AND HE STARTED HIS MEDITATION. BUT BEFORE HE SAT DOWN, HE HAD NO TIMEPIECE, NO WATCH, NO CALENDAR, AND SO HOW WAS HE GOING TO KNOW TWENTY-ONE DAYS? SO, HE GATHERED TWENTY-ONE SMALL ROCKS OR STONES AND THEN PILED IT IN FRONT OF HIM. AND THEN HE STARTED HIS MEDITATION, AND SO HE SAID, "THIS IS THE FIRST DAY." AND THEN HE THREW ONE ROCK AWAY. AND THAT IS HOW HE COUNTED HIS DAYS? HE EXPECTED SOME KIND OF A PHENOMENA BUT HE DIDN'T 'T KNOW WHAT. HE DIDN'T KNOW WHAT TO EXPECT. AND ALL THIS TIME DR. USUI, VERY FAITHFULLY, HE READ THE SCRIPTURES, CHANTED, MEDITATED, AND THEN? AND THEN EVERY DAY CAME, THEN ANOTHER DAY. FINALLY CAME THE MORNING OF THE TWENTY-FIRST, THAT WAS EARLY MORNING. AND HE SAID, "THE DARKEST OF NIGHT IS IN THE EARLIEST OF MORNING, BEFORE SUNRISE IS THE DARKEST".

THAT'S HOW HE DID THIS. THERE WAS NOT EVEN ONE STAR, NO MOON, OR ANY KIND OF A LIGHT. HE SAID THE SKY WAS DARK, JUST AS DARK AS IT COULD BE. AND WHEN HE FINISHED HIS MEDITATION AND HE SAID HE OPENED HIS EYES AND LOOKED INTO THE DARK SKY, AND ALL HE WAS THINKING WAS, "THIS IS MY LAST MEDITATION." AND THEN HE SAW A FLICKER OF LIGHT ONLY LARGE AS CANDLELIGHT, IN THE DARK. AND THEN HE SAID, "OH NOW, THIS PHENOMENON VERY STRANGE, BUT," HE SAID, "IT IS HAPPENING AND I AM NOT GOING TO EVEN SHUT MY EYES, OR, I SHALL OPEN MY EYES AS WIDE AS I CAN, AND TO WITNESS WHAT HAPPENS TO THE LIGHT."

AND THE LIGHT BEGINS TO MOVE VERY FAST TOWARDS HIM. THEN HE SAID, "OH, THE LIGHT! NOW I HAVE A CHANCE TO

"SHUT THE LIGHT, OR DODGE. WHAT SHALL I DO?" THEN HE SAID, "EVEN IF THE LIGHT STRIKES ME, AND IF I FALL, OR IF I DROP BACK, OR I MIGHT BURN." HE SAID," THIS IS THE BEST", HE SAID, " I AM NOT GOING TO RUN AWAY, I'M GOING TO FACE IT". AND WHEN HE FACED IT, HE BEGAN TO BRACE HIMSELF MORE, AND TO SAY, "COME, HIT ME, I AM READY." AND WITH THAT, HE RELAXED AND, WITH EYES WIDE OPEN, HE SAW THE LIGHT STRIKE IN THE CENTRE OF HIS FOREHEAD. HE FELL BACKWARD BECAUSE THE FORCE WAS SO GREAT. THEN HE SAID, "I DIED, BECAUSE I HAVE NO SENSE, NO FEELING, AND MY EYES WERE OPEN BUT I COULDN'T SEE". AND THEN HE SAID, "I DON'T KNOW HOW LONG, HOW MANY MINUTES I WAS DOWN, BUT" HE SAID", WHEN I AWOKE, THAT LIGHT WAS GONE AND FAR AWAY, I COULD HEAR THE ROOSTERS CROWING AND SO I KNEW IT WOULD BE DAWN PRETTY SOON."

THEN HE HAPPENED TO LOOK A LITTLE TO THE RIGHT SIDE AND HE SAW FROM THE RIGHT SIDE OF HIS FACE MILLIONS AND MILLIONS OF BUBBLES CAME OUT, BUBBLING UP, BUBBLING UP, BUBBLING UP, BUBBLING UP, MILLIONS AND MILLIONS AND MILLIONS OF BUBBLES. AND THESE BUBBLES ALL HAD COLOURS. AND THEY WERE THE COLOURS OF THE RAINBOW. AND, HE SAID, THEY DANCED IN FRONT OF HIM AND HE SAID HE WAS COUNTING THOSE COLOURS, AND IT HAD SEVEN COLOURS, ALL SEVEN."

In this extract Hawayo Takata explains that a great light struck Mikao Usui in the centre of the forehead, the location of the brow Chakra. What Takata suggests is synonymous with the idea of enlightenment. She goes on to say that all seven colours of the rainbow appeared before Mikao Usui. I find this of particular interest and later in the symbology section of this book, you will find out why!

"AND SO DR. USUI SAID, " THIS IS A PHENOMENON. I WAS BLESSED TODAY." THEN LAST OF ALL, HE SAW THE GREAT WHITE LIGHT COMING FROM THE RIGHT, AND THEN LIKE A SCREEN THEY JUST STOOD RIGHT IN FRONT OF HIM, LIKE A SCREEN. AND WHEN HE DREW HIS EYES TO THE SCREEN, HE

SAID, WHAT HE HAD STUDIED IN THE SANSKRIT, WHAT HE
SAW AND STUDIED IN THE SANSKRIT, HE SAID ONE BY ONE
FLEW OUT, AND THEN IN GOLDEN LETTERS, HE SAID THEY
JUST RADIATED OUT IN FRONT OF HIM AS IF TO SAY,
"REMEMBER! REMEMBER! "

Hawayo Takata continues to tell the well-known story of Mikao Usui descending the mountain on his 17-mile hike back to Kyoto on which he experienced 4 miracles. The first was his body felt strong despite not eating for 21 days. The second, he healed a badly cut toe after he stumbled. The third, he healed the toothache of the daughter of a snack bar owner. Finally, the fourth miracle was that he managed to eat a meal of rice, nori, salted cabbage and dried fish without experiencing indigestion. We pick up our story as he arrives at the temple to share his experience on Mount Kurama.

"HE KNOCKED AT THE DOOR. A LITTLE PAGEBOY CAME OUT.
AND HE SAID, "DR. USUI, WE ARE SO HAPPY THAT YOU ARE
HOME, BECAUSE IF YOU DID NOT COME HOME TONIGHT, YOU
KNOW WE WERE GOING TO SEND A SEARCHING PARTY
TOMORROW MORNING AS YOU REQUESTED." DR. USUI
SAID, "HOW IS OUR DEAR MONK?" "OH, HE'S SUFFERING
FROM ARTHRITIS, BACKACHE, AND THIS IS A COOL
EVENING, SO HE WAS HUGGING THE CHAPEL STOVE AND HE
WAS UNDER SILK COVERS."

HE SAID, "MY DEAR MONK, I AM BACK." THE FIRST THING
HE ASKED WAS "HOW WAS IT, HOW WAS YOUR
MEDITATION?"

"SUCCESS." THAT IS THE ONLY WORD HE COULD USE, WAS
SUCCESS.

AND THE MONK SAID, "OH, I FEEL SO HAPPY, I FEEL SO
HAPPY," HE SAID, "LET ME HEAR ABOUT IT."

Mikao Usui talked till late, recounting his experiences on the mountain and the next morning decided to experiment with Reiki by going to the slums in Kyoto to work with the beggars and the sick. Hawayo Takata talks of Mikao Usui working in the slums for seven years helping people to heal and sending them to the temple to get jobs. But one evening he found a familiar face, someone who he had helped and he had returned to the slums. Hawayo Takata explains that Mikao Usui felt he had failed and realised that he needed to heal the mind and spirit first then the body will be healed. This experience became the motivation for principles being added to the Reiki system.

"IF YOU ASK ME, WAS HE SUCCESSFUL? WAS HE A SUCCESS? FAR FROM IT, BECAUSE WHEN DR. USUI LEFT KYOTO AND HIS MINISTRY, HE LEFT IN SEARCH OF HOW TO HEAL THE PHYSICAL, HIS AIM WAS TO DO SOMETHING FOR THE BODY. SO HE FORGOT THE SPIRITUAL SIDE". HE BLAMED HIMSELF. HE SAID, "ALL THE CHURCHES IN KYOTO WERE RIGHT, THEY WERE RIGHT AND I WAS WRONG" HE BEGAN TO THINK AND HE SAID, "I FORGOT TO TEACH THEM BEFORE THEY LEFT, GRATITUDE".

SO THEREFORE, THE FIVE IDEALS WERE BORN AT THAT TIME. AND THE IDEALS ARE:

JUST FOR TODAY, DO NOT ANGER; JUST FOR TODAY, DO NOT WORRY; NUMBER THREE, WE SHALL COUNT OUR BLESSINGS AND HONOUR OUR FATHERS AND MOTHERS, AND OUR TEACHERS AND NEIGHBOURS; AND HONOUR OUR FOOD, WE SHALL NOT WASTE ANY FOOD, BECAUSE FOOD IS ALSO GOD-GIVEN, ALTHOUGH THE FARMERS CULTIVATE IT. BUT IF YOU DO HAVE FAMINE, YOU DO NOT HAVE FOOD. BUT WE JUST HAVE TO SHOW GRATITUDE TOWARDS FOOD. AND THEN, NUMBER FOUR, MAKE AN HONEST LIVING. WE HAVE TO WORK IN ORDER TO MAKE AN HONEST LIVING, THAT IS NUMBER FOUR. AND NUMBER FIVE IS TO BE KIND TO EVERYTHING THAT HAS LIFE. THESE ARE THE FIVE IDEALS OF REIKI, IT WAS BORN AT THAT INSTANT WHEN DR. USUI RECOGNISED HIS FAILURE. AND SO HE SAID, "IF I HAD TAUGHT THEM THE SPIRITUAL SIDE OF IT FIRST, AND THEN HEALED THE BODY, IT WOULD HAVE BEEN EFFECTIVE." AND THAT IS WHEN DR. USUI WALKED OUT OF THE COMPOUND [SLUMS] AND THEN HE MADE A PILGRIMAGE

ALL OVER JAPAN, YOU KNOW THE MAIN ISLAND PART FROM THE NORTH TO THE SOUTH ON FOOT. AND HE CHOSE A BIG MALL, AND HE TOOK A TORCH, AND LIGHTED THE TORCH AND HE WOULD BE WALKING UP AND DOWN THE MALL WHERE THERE WERE THOUSANDS OF PEOPLE. SO, ONE YOUNG MAN CAME TO HIM, AND HE SAID, "MY DEAR MONK, IF YOU ARE LOOKING FOR LIGHT," HE SAID, "YOU DON'T NEED THAT TORCH. TODAY WE HAVE A LOT OF SUNSHINE. THIS IS A BEAUTIFUL DAY," HE SAID. "YOU DON'T NEED THIS TORCH LIGHT." HE SAID, "WE CAN SEE."

USUI SAID, "YES, THAT IS VERY TRUE. BUT, I AM LOOKING AND SEARCHING FOR PEOPLE THAT HAVE VERY SAD, DEPRESSED MINDS. PEOPLE WHO ARE UNHAPPY. I AM SEARCHING FOR PEOPLE THAT NEED THIS LIGHT TO BRIGHTEN THEIR HEARTS AND TO TAKE AWAY THEIR DEPRESSION, AND CLEANSE THEIR CHARACTER AND THEIR MIND AND BODY. AND SO, IF YOU WANT TO HEAR THIS LECTURE, COME TO THE CHURCH."

It was during this time whilst Mikao Usui was travelling around Japan that Chujiro Hayashi a retired reserve in the Imperial Navy first encountered him at a lecture he was giving.

"DR. USUI KIND OF POINTED HIM OUT AFTER THE LECTURE, AND HE SAID, "I SEE THAT YOU ARE A MAN THAT IS A LEADER." HE SAID, "YES, I AM. I HAVE JUST SERVED MY TIME AS A NAVY COMMANDER IN THE IMPERIAL MAJESTY'S FORCE. AND NOW, I AM A RESERVE IN THE NAVY, SO I HAVE EARNED ALL THAT."

SO HE [USUI] SAID," BUT YOU ARE TOO YOUNG TO RETIRE. SO WHY DO YOU NOT JOIN ME IN THIS CRUSADE, THEN TO HELP PEOPLE? I THINK YOU WOULD BE A VERY GOOD PERSON TO DO THIS." AND SO DR. HAYASHI SAID, "WELL, I WILL TRY. IF YOU RECOMMEND IT, I AM INTERESTED. "AND AT THAT TIME, DR. HAYASHI WAS ONLY FORTY- FIVE. AND SO HE WALKED WITH DR. USUI ALL OVER. HE SAID THAT HE WAS WITH HIM, I DON'T KNOW, I FORGOT HOW MANY YEARS, BUT UNTIL DR. USUI DIED, WENT INTO TRANSITION,

AND WHEN HE DID, AND HE SAID DR. USUI ANNOUNCED THAT IT WAS DR. CHUJIRO HAYASHI THAT WAS GOING TO CONTINUE THIS USUI SYSTEM IN THE ART OF HEALING. THIS IS THE LIFE STORY OF DR. USUI, WHICH I HAVE HEARD FROM DR. HAYASHI. AND DURING HIS REIGN, DR. HAYASHI NEVER CHANGED THE SYSTEM. IT IS THE SAME TODAY, AND MY STUDENTS, AND MY FOLLOWERS, LEARNED THIS ART OF HEALING AT THE USUI REIKI RYOHO. IN ENGLISH, IT IS THE USUI SYSTEM IN THE ART OF HEALING. REIKI IS A JAPANESE WORD, BUT IN ENGLISH IT IS UNIVERSAL LIFE ENERGY. BUT I USE THE WORD REIKI BECAUSE I LEARNED IN JAPAN, AND THEREFORE I STILL CONTINUE TO USE THE SHORT WORD REIKI."

HAWAYO TAKATA 1979

PART 3.

REIKI SYMBOLS

THE ENCODED MESSAGE

"The artist is meant to put the objects of this world together in such a way that through them you will experience that light, that radiance which is the light of our consciousness and which all things both hide and when properly looked upon, reveal."

Joseph Campbell

The second and third levels of Reiki introduce four symbols into the system. These are often referred to as the golden keys, which suggests that they are there to open doors. Symbolism is a powerful way to communicate the essence of something. Similar symbols appear in diverse cultures in different parts of the world with no obvious anthropological connection but have the same meaning. Some symbols have been given different connotations through historical association and context. For example, the swastika, originally used as a symbol of good fortune and prosperity in Hindu, Buddhist and Native American cultures, was hijacked by the Nazis. Today it is illegal to have the swastika on display in Germany due to the negative associations to it. If you were to Google map Japan and zoom in, you will see thousands of swastikas, each one being used to mark a sacred temple or place of worship. There is even one marking the Kuramadera temple at Mount Kurama where Mikao Usui is said to have discovered Reiki.

Symbols are encrypted with layers of information, often with elements that remain concealed until we are ready to see them. Some view them as training wheels, used to awaken knowledge and develop deeper understanding. The process of being with a symbol can reveal its hidden depths and it is beneficial to sit with them, meditate upon them and notice how they affect us. It is intriguing how students, given the Reiki symbols for the first time, intuitively get a sense of what they signify and represent. It is extraordinary the depths of insight they often have.

We find variations in how the symbols are drawn, in much the same way we find variations in a person's signature. It is impossible to sign our own signature in the same way twice, so it is unsurprising that the symbols appear as varied as they do. I will not be concentrating on their form here, instead I would like to take the time to look into the story they tell us and discover why Mikao Usui included them in his practice. As I look into the varying hypotheses that already exist and introduce my own, I hope to give an insight into how they convey deep spiritual meaning and represent the steps we must take to awaken our essential nature.

I have often thought, what if the Reiki symbols told a deeper story and were not simply there as arbitrary tools to aid our practice? What if their presence and inclusion in the system was to help students develop a fundamental understanding of their own spiritual nature. What if they held clues to the evolution and migration of spiritual practices that informed and inspired Mikao Usui? What if the symbols have a relationship to each other and encoded in them is information that relates to an ancient story that is consistent with nearly every story of creation ever told?

I am going to explain what they have revealed to me over the years, in particular the symbiotic relationship between them, and like a map that leads to treasure, I will share what I have found of their deeper meaning and significance. I believe two of the symbols are archetypal in the sense that they define the human story and explain our function in relation to the rest of the cosmos, connecting us to ancient mythological concepts. The others offer an approach to support the journey and reveal to us the ultimate goal, enlightenment.

As Reiki is an unfolding process and so too is awareness, this in no way represents a complete understanding of the symbols, in fact I would be disappointed if it did. I would like you to view it more as a meandering journey down an unknown river that may or may not arrive at a satisfactory conclusion. As I ponder the results of my own meditations, think of me 'talking out loud' and sharing my own observations. Like any journey down a river the excitement is in not quite knowing what awaits us around the next bend and I urge you to read the following with all that in mind.

As far as I can tell from my research, the Reiki symbols all existed prior to their inclusion in the Reiki system. Certainly they have been in the public domain since first being published in 1992 by A.J. MacKenzie in his book: 'The Challenge To Teach Reiki'. For this reason, and because of the associations I need to communicate clearly, I took the decision to reproduce the Reiki symbols as drawn by Hawayo Takata in this book.

SYMBOL 1.

THE POWER SYMBOL

MANTRA CHO KU REI (CKR)

TRANSLATION - CHOKU - DIRECT REI - SPIRITS

HAWAYO TAKATA TRANSLATED IT AS "PUT THE POWER HERE"

CHOKUREI CAN ALSO MEAN AN 'IMPERIAL COMMAND'.

The journey through the three symbols at 2nd level usually begins with the power symbol. Its mantra is Cho Ku Rei (CKR)

Like most things in the Reiki community, you will find various different forms of this symbol. Hawayo Takata drew it starting from top left to right, then down through the vertical line and finally spiralling anticlockwise into the centre. There are alternatives you can find which sometimes have the symbol appearing as a mirror image to the one here, starting from top right with the spiral moving clockwise into the centre. This, as far as I know, is not an original variation of this symbol.

'Rei', we know, forms part of our pictograph for Reiki. As we have discovered, it tells the story of the Wu shaman performing ceremonial rituals, like praying and dancing for rain. They offered crystal jade, [heaven's essence] to the gods so they could receive heaven's blessings as rain to nourish their crops.

Viewed from a more psycho-spiritual perspective, these ceremonies were about calling on 'The Great Bright Light' to infuse mind, body and spirit. In this sense, Reiki is a shamanistic path, calling upon and surrendering to a higher spiritual power. 'Rei', is the ancient laws, the ceremony, the universal spirit and the path to Enlightenment. Incidentally, in biblical texts Rei means my shepherd, my companion.

The Japanese five-element system of earth, water, fire, air and space [void] may well help us to better understand the process by which energy manifestation rituals took place. When the Shamans invoked Great Spirit to enlighten their ceremonies, they first created a sacred space [cast a sacred wheel] by honouring the cardinal directions. Earth, Water, Fire and Air would be represented and placed in their relevant directions. Linked together they signified a sacred space of perfect balance and harmony into which universal energy could be manifest. The shaman would then be able to direct energy to where it was needed.

The three components in the formation of the Power symbol are as follows. The first stroke symbolises heaven and is associated to the element of Consciousness. The second stroke symbolises the vertical line that connects heaven to earth and is associated to the element of Light emerging from the Void. The spiral into the centre symbolises the four elements earth, water, fire and air, moving anticlockwise.

In the book "Vital Breath of the Dao" by Zhongxian Wu, there is an interesting reference to the character for shaman, 'Wu'. He says, that the character Wu depicts Si fang – four directions or four quadrants. He explains the Wu shaman applied the concept of 4 quadrants to their own bodies, the heart being the centre. The character he used for Wu was different to ones I had seen before and is as follows.

WU- SHAMAN

So if we say, the shaman's role was to bring 'Great Spirit' from heaven to earth as 'The Great Bright Light' to manifest in the physical world. Could CKR be a visual representation of that journey? The elements of 'Consciousness' and 'Light' being brought out of the 'Void' represented by the first two strokes? Their manifestation on earth as the elements 'Earth', 'Water', 'Fire' & 'Air' represented by the anticlockwise spiral spinning into the centre?

Does the combination of these seven elements represent our interaction between the physical and the spiritual worlds? If so, is the CKR a key to unlock the gateway between worlds? The question arises; is CKR simply a vehicle for the manifestation of spirit on earth or does it also reveal our potentiality? Does it exemplify the journey of transformation so immortalised by ancient alchemists in their desire to elevate themselves and reach up to embody spirit?

Reiki researcher James Deacon found references to the term cho ku rei in the writings of Masahisa Goi, founder of the new religious group Byakkō

Shinkōkai. Goi who had been sickly since birth, had been restored to health using a healing practice called Johrei [purification of the spirit] developed by Mokichi Okada in the 1930's. In his book 'The Future of Mankind', Goi writes:

"In the beginning, Great God took His body, His light, and divided it into various rays of light. He then functioned 7 rays of light to operate as the power source of human beings. These 7 rays of origin, which I call Chokurei (direct spirits from God), are the image of God working in this world of mankind."

Is the idea that [Great God] fashioned 7 rays of origin to create the physical universe and everything in it, a reflection of the 7 elements that make up our existence? Or is there an even more profound story encoded within this symbol?

It is perhaps surprising how little has been uncovered about the CKR, especially as, when first shown this symbol many find it strangely familiar. In keeping with the essence of this book let's allow the flow to take us where it will, head downstream, permit the current to take us and find what is around the next corner.

When I was a three-year old boy, I lived in Swaziland in South Africa and being adventurous, I was always digging about in the garden. One day my father came out of the house to find me face to face with a cobra coiled and ready to strike. My father. unable to do anything, could only watch and pray. Fortunately, I just stayed very still until the cobra retreated back into the long grass and I escaped unscathed. Some have suggested that CKR represents a coiled serpent with its head raised ready to strike and is therefore linked to Chakra theory. 'The Kundalini Serpent' energy in Chakra theory is coiled at the base of the spine and rises through the Chakras as consciousness is developed. Snakes, like spirals, have permeated ancient mythological concepts for millennia and as the spiral is recognisable within our CKR, I have decided it would be the best place for me to start. As I follow the flow and allow things to unfold I will wait to see if our friend the snake reappears.

The spiral is found throughout the world from ancient civilization to the modern day. In the film 'The Jungle Book' you may well remember 'Mowgli' was hypnotised by the python, 'Kaa's', spiralling eyes. As Mowgli discovered, spirals have associations to being entranced [in trance]. The word entrance also suggests a gateway. The Celtic artists believed the simple act of creating a spiral freed their minds allowing them to access creative consciousness. Spiritually the spiral symbolises the movement between the inner creative and the outer manifest worlds. Spirals mark growth from within and the movement of life force into expression. In China, the spiral was an early symbol for the sun until 'Empress Wu' of the Tang dynasty, decreed the swastika be used as the symbol for the sun instead. But before we open the proverbial can of worms that is the ancient swastika let me share an interesting piece of information with you; the ancient Sumerian name for 'snake' is derived from the word 'sun' – 'sun-ake'.

THE SPIRAL AND THE SWASTIKA

If we are able to put aside the association the swastika had with Nazi Germany, we will discover that along with the spiral, it is one of the most spontaneously occurring symbols found throughout ancient civilisations. It appears right around the globe from Native American cultures to India. The earliest archaeological evidence of a swastika motif dates back to 10,000 BC found on a mammoth's tusk in the Ukraine.

The swastika is the first of the 65 auspicious symbols associated with the footprint of the Buddha. It is said to contain the whole mind of the Buddha and can often be found imprinted on the chest, feet or palms of

Buddha images. Throughout Asia it marks sacred temples and is seen as a symbol of good fortune, eternity, abundance, prosperity and long life. Esoterically, the swastika is seen as representing Buddhahood itself or the immaculate Heart of Buddha and is called Sin-Yin (Heart Seal).

THE HEART SEAL

The swastika used in Japan is known as a manji (whirlwind), and represents Dharma, universal harmony and the balance of opposites. The manji made up of a vertical and horizontal axis is said to represent the unification of opposites [Yin and Yang] in all four directions. The centre point is balanced through the spiraling forces created by the interaction of these elements.

The swastika is related to the elements, each of the four arms represents an element in rotation around the centre. Swastikas can be found both right handed and left handed and there appears some ambiguity as to which direction it is meant to spin. Some have said that when the arms face to the left it is radiating light and when the arms face to the right it is receiving light. For this reason in Buddhism, it is often depicted as left facing.

In China, it is said to have come from heaven. One of the Chinese names for the swastika is Wan meaning the ten thousand things, the "Great Number", signifying the whole of creation. I sometimes wonder if Hawayo Takata set the price to become a Reiki master at $10,000 because at the time in the USA it was the cost of a house, or because as a number it had greater significance? I am sure she would have known 10,000 is the 'number of creation'.

According to Taoist tradition, the ruler of the manifest universe was a deity figure well known in Chinese popular culture called the Jade Emperor. He is said to be the Great Heavenly Emperor of the Supreme Palace of Polaris [The Northern Star]. From there he sends Qi, the Heavenly Breath, streaming down, connecting Heaven and Earth and infusing mankind with vitality. It is no wonder then that the ancient Wu shaman considered jade to be heaven's essence and offered it to the Gods in their rituals. Lets not forget that choku rei also refers to an 'Imperial command.'

Polaris [the northern star], is historically the most important heavenly body in the visible night sky. It is a constant on our horizon around which everything spirals because the axis of the earth points directly at it. Explorers have seen it as their great [*] companion, using it to navigate and tell the time. They knew, providing they were in the northern hemisphere, if they traveled towards Polaris, they would be heading north.

[*] *In biblical texts Rei means my shepherd or my companion.*

To find the northern star, we first need to locate the big dipper, so called because it resembles a giant ladle. Incidentally the Chinese call it the [Jade] Emperor's Chariot because it demonstrated his control of the four directions as it revolved around Polaris in the centre.

POLARIS AND THE BIG DIPPER

Once you have located the Big Dipper, look at the two outermost stars that form part of the ladle head, opposite of the handle. If you imagine a line connecting these two stars, and extend that line up and beyond, the next star you will encounter (roughly five times the height of the ladle head) will be Polaris, the North Star.

So why am I going on about soup ladles and the North Star, when I should be discussing CKR you might ask? Well, just as the sun and moon appear to rise in the east and set in the west due to the rotation of the earth, so do the stars. If you were to take a time-lapse photograph of the night sky with the lens pointing at the north star, you would see the big dipper rotating anticlockwise around it a bit like the spiral in our CKR. Astronomers, navigators and farmers have used the earth's rotation around the Polaris to keep track of the stars, the time and the seasons. On the solstices and equinoxes throughout the year, the big dipper marks the cardinal directions, so not only does this constellation point us to true north but it also reflects the seasons of our yearly calendar.

If we illustrate the big dipper's movement around Polaris on the equinoxes and solstices it appears to resemble the swastika. Farm tools in India till today have the swastika drawn on them, with a prayer "May your good harvest be as regular as the rotation of the stars." In the UK the big dipper is called 'The Plough' because not only is it shaped like a plough, but its position in the sky was used to determine agrarian planting and harvesting seasons.

THE FOUR SEASONS

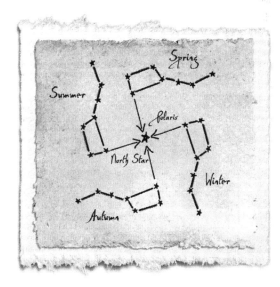

So with the swastika's historical association to a point in the universe that we could rely upon, it is unsurprising that early aviators used to sew it onto their jackets as a sign of good fortune. They were unknowingly referring to the great navigational aid in the heavens. The swastika was sewn onto airmen's jackets, symbolising they could always find their way home by following true north. I find it fascinating that one of the many uses for the CKR symbol is as a seal or amulet of protection.

It may be worth remembering at this point that on Mount Kurama, the early Tendai monks placed a shrine to Bishamonten who was known as 'The Protector of the North'. Is there a definitive relationship between the 'Deity' and 'North Star' as the great protector? Could it also be that encoded within the spirals of CKR is the path that leads us home?

Despite suggestions that the Chakra system is not part of traditional Reiki, I cannot help notice the seven elements of the Chakras are reflected in the CKR. When referring to the CKR symbol, one of Hawayo Takatas masters Mary Mcfayden said, *"Draw at least three circles to give 7 cut points on the downward line, these cut points represent the main Chakras."*

Hawayo Takata's translation of CKR was, "to put the power here!" Is it just coincidence that if we were to draw a large CKR over the body through the Chakra system, the spiral would lead straight to the heart? I have taught students for many years to open a treatment in this way. At the end of the treatment drawing it in reverse from the centre of the spiral outwards, in effect returning the elements back to the heavens.

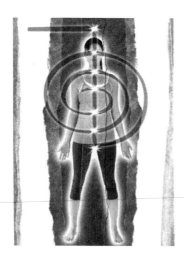

CKR THROUGH THE CHAKRAS

There is an old French illustration called the L'Homme Terrestre Naturel Tenebreux, which shows a similar idea albeit clockwise and depicting just four elements. Notice the coiled snake around the sun in the place of the heart!

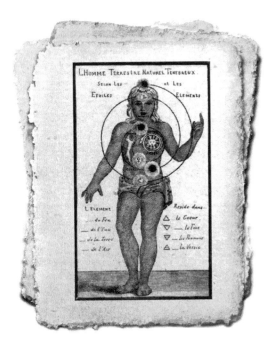

L'HOMME TERRESTRE NATUREL

So where has the flow taken us so far? Does CKR reveal our intrinsic connection to the essential elements of creation that like the Wu shaman, we can call upon, gather, harness and bring into balance? Does it metaphorically signify the gateway between earth and the heaven, where the Jade Emperor ruler of the manifest universe and his supreme palace in the northern star resides? Does drawing CKR ask 'Great Spirit' to entrance us, invoking 'The Great Bright Light' to infuse mind and body? Has it evolved from ancient psycho spiritual concepts that can be traced back via the swastika, the spiral and the snake to the sun? Is the spiral found within our power symbol a representation of the expansion and contraction to and from singularity? Does it represent a path that when followed will take us home?

SPIRAL, SNAKE, SUN, SWASTIKA – CKR?

To fully answer these questions, I first need to introduce symbol 2 to you! But before I do, let me share some of the findings of researcher James Deacon. He discovered a link between Choku Rei and Nao Hi [which also means direct spirit] from the Omoto belief. He compiled quotes from a four-part work by Onisaboro Deguchi, entitled 'Divine Signposts'. Two of those quotes reflect my own understanding; that when I open the gateway to Great Spirit, my heart becomes God's heart and the body and soul functions fully and shines with the beautiful light of Beingness.

"God endows human beings with naohi and thereby He gives the human soul limitless power. Thus does the body and soul of those in whom naohi functions fully shine with a beautiful light."

"If you are favored with naohi, your prayer to God becomes certain and true happiness can be yours, because your heart conforms to God's heart."

I found similar concepts related to the swastika in the writings of Zelia Nuttall an American anthropologist 1857 – 1933.

"It is the Alpha and the Omega of universal creative force, evolving from pure Spirit and ending in gross Matter. It is also the key to the cycle of Science, divine and human; and he who comprehends its full meaning is for ever liberated from the toils of Mahamaya, the great Illusion and Deceiver."

"WHEN THE DALAI LAMA APPEARS IN PUBLIC
FOR THE PURPOSE OF TEACHING,
THERE IS A PEACOCK FEATHER,
A CLEAR CRYSTAL
AND A SMALL ROUND MIRROR PRESENT.
THESE SYMBOLISE THE NATURE OF THE MIND
AND OUR POTENTIALITY AS BEINGS OF LIGHT."

SYMBOL 2.

THE MENTAL EMOTIONAL SYMBOL

MANTRA SEI HEKI (SHK)

TRANSLATION - SEI - EMOTIONAL HEKI - CALMNESS

HAWAYO TAKATA USED IT FOR 'THE HABIT TREATMENT'

The second symbol on our journey at 2nd level is the mental/emotional symbol. Its mantra is Sei Heki [SHK] The purpose of its inclusion in the system of Reiki is as a vehicle to help purify the mind and calm emotions. A specific healing practice is associated with this symbol that Hawayo Takata referred to as 'The Habit Treatment'.

It has been suggested, like CKR, this symbol represents our relationship between heaven and earth. 'Great Spirit' and mankind becoming one, and I have often questioned if there is a symbiotic relationship between CKR and SHK? If so, what way do the two symbols relate and if Usui was leaving clues, what was he telling us by including these symbols in his system of Reiki? Let us meander down the Reiki river and see where it takes us!

How Mikao Usui came to be inspired by this symbol and incorporate it in the Reiki system is not completely clear to me. In a recording made by Hawayo Takata in 1979 she said,

"[Mikao Usui] went into studying the Sanskrit, and when he later studied very hard to master it, he found a formula. Just as plain as day, nothing hard but very simple. Like two and two equals four, three and three equals six, as simple as that. And so he said, "Very well, I've found it. Now, I have to try to interpret this, because it was written 2500 years ago".

She went on to say, *"The Japanese characters that are written in the sutras, all these characters, originally they came from China. He [Mikao Usui] went deep into the Chinese characters and became a master of the Chinese characters. And after that was completed, he said, "Not enough", he said. "After all, Buddha was a Hindu, and therefore "he said, "I should study the Sanskrit."*

So what was this simple formula he found hidden in the Sanskrit sutras? Is there a clue in the symbology he left for us? If you remember, the temple on Mount Kurama where he is reported to have received Reiki was under Tendai control up until 1949. Within the temple there are symbols called 'shuji' that represent a triad of spiritual deities. One of these shuji 'Kiriku' characterizes in this case the Buddhist Deity Senju Kannon.

It has largely been accepted by the Reiki community that SHK and the shuji character 'Kiriku' are one and the same. Furthermore 'Kiriku' is said to relate to the older Sanskrit seed syllable 'Hirih'. It represents 'The Pure

Land' Buddhist deity for compassion Amitābha who sits in the western sky. Some consider Amitābha to be synonymous with Amitayus, the Buddha of Infinite Life. Amitayus is usually depicted holding a vessel of the elixir of immortal life and an ashoka-tree, representing the union of the spiritual and the material. Amitābha and Amida Butsu are one and the same and in the Mikkyo esoteric Buddhist tradition this Buddhist deity is known as Amida Nyorai. To avoid confusion I shall refer to this Deity simply as Amida.

HRIH KIRIKU

Seed syllables or shuji characters are traditionally used as meditation tools, drawn on large scrolls and hung in places of worship as a focal point for contemplation. Meditating upon a seed syllable and chanting its mantra is a way to invoke the deity that it represents. In Buddhist meditations there is the Amida mantra 'Om amitabha hrih' or sometimes [Om Amideva Hrih] with the seed syllable 'Hrih' at the end. Calling the name of Amitabha Buddha to purify and transmute the poisons of the mind.

Amida is often depicted with Senju Kannon who together welcome the souls of the dying into 'The Pure Lands' a place that provided a stepping stone towards enlightenment and liberation from the eternal cycle of rebirth. Ancients believed a pair of peacocks guarded the gates of paradise and both Amida and Senju Kannon are often seen with this sacred animal. Amida is often depicted sitting in a meditation posture, upon a peacock with hands in the mida-no-jouin Mudra. This hand position offers a clue to the stillness and balance that can be found within. Senju Kannon is depicted with a thousand arms and a thousand eyes, enabling him to see all distress and act to alleviate it with a compassionate embrace.

MIDA-NO-JOUIN MUDRA

So where did the emphasis for the purification of mind and emotions associated to the SHK symbol come from? Let us go deeper into the mysteries of ancient mythology surrounding our peacock and see what it reveals. The peacock is famous for displaying its tail train and naturally replaces its feathers annually and for this reason is often seen as a symbol of renewal. In fact two peacocks drinking from a chalice symbolise rebirth. Peacocks are considered sacred in India where the feathers may be burnt to ward off disease. The peacock feather is often kept in the home to help safe guard the energy in the environment. Peacock feathers are marked distinctly with thousands of eyes and in some cultures they represent the 'All Seeing Eye'. The peacock is also a solar symbol because the circular fan of the tail in full display resembles the sun. The peacock has the ability to eat poisonous snakes without harm. In Indian folklore it is said that the peacock's brilliant colours actually come from the poison of the snakes they eat. The poisons when ingested transmuted into beauty. The shimmering colours of his tail feathers created by transforming snake venom into solar iridescence. The practice of meditating and invoking Amida is said to transform the poisons of the mind into the full beauty and splendour of the astral body.

The peacock is also credited with an ability to neutralise a highly toxic plant known as "wolf-bane," used in Asia as a treatment for mental illness. In many cultures it stands for the incorruptibility and immortality of the soul and has been attributed with the power of resurrection. Many believe the mythical phoenix actually evolved from the legend of the peacock!

Let us pause for a moment and drift. As we do, let me share with you a revelation of my own that occurred one dark February evening whilst I was sitting in my office staring at my computer screen. I had loads of images spread all over the desktop of Buddhist deities and as I sat there looking at them, I noticed something captivating! The thousand-armed and thousand-eyed Senju Kannon looked just like a peacock displaying its tail feathers! Intrigued I started to look at other Deities associated to the peacock. What I found was a litany of associated deities that read like a mythological tale, running right back through time. Just a very few of the deities I found related to the peacock were;

> AMIDA NYORAI, SENJU KANNON,
> LORD KARTTIKEYA, SUBRAMANYA,
> KUJYAKU, MARUGAN,
> SANAT KUMARA,
> ARCHANGEL MICHAEL,
> KING MELCHIZEDEK,
> DIONYSUS,
> QUETZLCOATL,
> ENKI,
> KRISHNA.

PEACOCK DEITIES

In Japan there is 'Kojaku-o' the 'Peacock King' who rides a peacock and has four arms. He is known as the 'Rain God' [Remember Reiki and its relationship to the rainmakers?] The mythical founder of the Shugendo order 'En-No-Gyoja' practiced the magical formula of Kojaku-o the 'Peacock King' and is said to have changed into a phoenix and flown to heaven itself. The name Shugendo refers to a spiritual path [do] where the development of spiritual and magical power [gen] is achieved by retreating into the mountains and performing magical practices [shu]. It is an ancient tradition influenced by Taoist, esoteric Buddhist and shamanic practices where mountains are regarded as places of supernatural power.

TAWSI MELEK

In Persia 'The Peacock King' was known as Tawsi Melek and was the most important deity of the Yezidis who believe they possess the oldest religion in the world. They believe Tawsi Melek was the first to emerge from the 'Light of God' in the form of a 'Seven-Rayed Rainbow' around the 'Sun'. Tawsi Melek is accompanied by six great angels [archangels?] that collectively formed the seven colours of the rainbow. Let us remember what Masahisa Goi wrote

"In the beginning, Great God took His body, His light, and divided it into various rays of light. He then functioned 7 rays of light to operate as the power source of human beings. These 7 rays of origin, which I call Chokurei (direct spirits from God), are the image of God working in this world of mankind

In the Meshefê Re, the Yezidi's "Black Book," there is a passage that describes the seven great angels. The text states that the supreme god created a pearl containing the substance of the physical universe. For forty thousand years this pearl sat upon a primal bird, which was an embryonic form of Tawsi Melek which then divided into the seven great angels. Once the seven great angels were created, they produced the earth out of the substance in the original pearl. The earth remained barren and shook with violent earthquakes and volcanic activity. The supreme god sent the peacock angel to sedate the earth and cover it with flora and fauna. As Tawsi Melek descended into the physical dimension his seven-colored rainbow self became manifest as a magnificent bird of seven colors, the peacock. He flew around the globe in order to bless every part of it. With the earth in a more placid phase of its evolution the great angels proceeded to their next creation, Adam, the first human. Tawsi Melek transmitted the breath of life into him. When Adam rose to his feet, Tawsi Melek quickly swung him around to face the sun and told him that there was something much greater than he and that praying daily to the sun as a form of the supreme god would help him to remember this truth. Melek gave prayers in 72 languages for his 72 sons and 72 who would populate the countries of the earth. The peacock angel informed Adam that if he and his descendants remained steadfast in righteousness they would eventually see and know the supreme god personally. In the meantime, Tawsi Melek would be their protector and teacher from another dimension."

In Vajrayana Buddhism the 'Peacock King' is known as 'Mahamayuri' and is regarded as having a subtle body of limitless form. What this means is many Buddhist deities are emanations of 'The Peacock King' in particular Amida. It is also believed that in a previous life, Gautama Buddha [the founder of Buddhism], reincarnated as the 'Peacock King'. There is a Buddhist empowerment sutra 'Mahamayuri Dharani' [The Peacock King Sutra] which is said to cure all sicknesses and it is alleged Gautama Buddha chanted it with great devotion.

Even Maoson one of the "Spiritual Kings of the World celebrated today by the Kurama- kokyo sect has a similar legend to ascended master Sanat Kamara, who is said to have come from the bright star, [Venus] as a 16 year old boy with 'peacock feathers' growing from his hind and of all the possible places where he could have chosen to alight, decided upon Mount Kurama!

So with so much information to digest let us return to my opening question at the beginning of this chapter. In what way do the symbols SHK and CKR relate and if Usui was leaving clues, what was he telling us by including these symbols in the system of Reiki?

Interestingly as I am sure you suspected, we find the re appearance of our old friend the snake! Let us recall the peacock eats snakes and is immune to its poison. Throughout this book, we have discovered the shamanic roots of Reiki. Many of the psycho-spiritual concepts that have arisen are due to the migration of ancient myths and legends that use animals to explain their beliefs. In fact, many of the asanas in Yoga and movements in Qigong are based on animals. Yoga has asanas for both the peacock and the cobra, as does Qigong. The cobra represents transformation. When it is on its belly it can only see from an earthly perspective but when it rises up above the material world it gains a higher perspective and realises its greater purpose!

If the associations made between 'Hrih', 'Kiriku' and 'SHK' are true and the SHK symbol is connected to the peacock. It may well be the suggestion CKR is a coiled snake with its head raised is more accurate than people at first realised. What if all along Mikao Usui included these two symbols in our map because he understood the mythological relationship between the coiled snake and the peacock? Do these two archetypal symbols not reflect the duality of our earthbound nature and our potential as incarnate spiritual beings?

The ancient alchemists believed the negative distorted aspects of one's self, unless purified would dominate. So through the purification of the mind, is not our full potentiality revealed? Are we symbolically transforming snake venom into solar iridescence? The triumph of wisdom over poisonous tendencies, the Kundalini 'serpent' energy rising up, into the full beauty and splendour of the radiant peacocks tail?

BODHISATTVA

In Buddhism an enlightened being that is motivated by great compassion towards all sentient beings is known as a Bosatsu in Japan or a Bodhisattva in Sanskrit. They are often depicted riding on the backs of peacocks with snakes underfoot, because just like a peacock can transform snake poison into beauty so too can a bosatsu transform ignorance and negativity into an enlightened state of mind.

Let us remember the word, 'snake', is derived from both the animal and the sun – sun-ake and the stylized spirals and swastikas that evolved from the serpent were used as symbols for the sun. The ancient Taoists developed the concept that every human was a microscosmic reflection of the greater macrocosm. Therefore, the snake was not only symbolic of the creative life force that flowed through us but also represented our internal sun. So within the myths and legends of sun-ake, the human potential to become en-light-ened is revealed.

COULD SYMBOL 1. BE THE SNAKE, REPRESENTING OUR JOURNEY FROM THE SEED OF CREATIVE POTENTIAL TO AWAKENED CONSCIOUSNESS EXPRESSED THROUGH THE 7 ELEMENTS EARTH, WATER, FIRE, AIR, SPACE, LIGHT AND CONSCIOUSNESS?

COULD SYMBOL 2. BE THE PEACOCK REPRESENTING, THE PURIFICATION AND TRANSFORMATIONAL POWER OF INNER ALCHEMY. MERGING OUR DUAL NATURE, OUR LOWER AND HIGHER SELVES INTO ONE RADIANT BEING?

In the context of our Reiki practice, we can view SHK as a symbol that represents our own spiritual metamorphosis, to be used to transform our state of mind. As the cause of our suffering is invariably the result of unsolicited thoughts being allowed to run riot, the SHK symbol can purify the mind, transmuting it's poisons and restoring us to a more resourceful inner state of peace and calm.

"YOU ARE NOT A DROP
IN THE OCEAN.

YOU ARE THE ENTIRE
OCEAN IN A DROP."

RUMI

SYMBOL 3.

THE ABSENT HEALING SYMBOL

MANTRA HON SHA ZE SHO NEN (HSZSN)

""THE ORIGIN OF ALL, THE ESSENCE OF
OUR BEING IS PURE CONSCIOUSNESS."

The third symbol on our journey at 2nd level is the distant healing or distant contact symbol. Its mantra is Hon Sha Ze Sho Nen (HSZSN). Its primary purpose in the Reiki system is to help contact someone or something that cannot be touched physically. The practice of distant healing; 'Sending Reiki through time and over distance' is therefore associated to this symbol. It has been suggested Hawayo Takata referred to it as 'The Telephone Dial'.

Assuming Mikao Usui was leaving clues for us to follow, what might be the deeper significance and motive for its inclusion in the Reiki system? Let's delve into the meaning of this symbol and find out why it has become synonymous with the practice of distant healing shall we?

The distant healing symbol is not strictly a symbol and rather like the character for Reiki, is a series of kanji characters combined together to form a pictograph. As was common practice in esoteric traditions, the kanji in this pictograph have been compressed together making the individual characters difficult to read. Nevertheless the pictograph reads like its mantra [HSZSN] and consequently they are one and the same. It appears the meaning of this pictograph is open to interpretation and many different translations have been suggested. Most focus on original nature, the essence of being, correct thought and consciousness.

Frans Stiene suggests;

"My original nature is a correct thought and I am correct consciousness".

Mary Mcfayden one of Hawayo Takata's masters translates it as;

"The God in me extends to the God in you."

Hyakuten Inamoto William Rand and Hiroshi Doi agreed the following translation had a satisfying degree of accuracy.

"The origin of all is pure consciousness."

James Deacon suggests, a meaningful translation could be;

"Correct thought is the essence of being"

As you can see, there is a degree of disparity between these translations. There is however a fundamental thread that runs through all of them. Original nature refers to one's Buddha nature. If we allow ourselves to loosen the constraints we have around that label for a moment and sense the deeper meaning, original nature could refer to our spirit, our divine nature or as Mary Mcfayden said, the God in me and you.

With that in mind, what clearly appears to me when I look at these translations is;

> "THE ORIGIN OF ALL, THE ESSENCE OF OUR BEING IS PURE CONSCIOUSNESS."

While writing this chapter, Dolly, our family dishwasher, washed its last dish. Dolly died! In a large family such as ours, Dolly was much loved, and an essential part of daily life. It was sadly time for an upgrade and I remembered a client who supplied and installed quality domestic appliances for a living. I hadn't seen him for years and thought I would look up his number and give him a call. Before I had the chance to call him, he rang me out of the blue that same afternoon! I don't know why I am still surprised when these things happen to me. I don't think he was really sure why he was calling, he was just responding to a telepathic telephone call, but I got a shiny new replacement for dear dead Dolly!

I believe part of the reason we are given symbol 3 is to help us understand this principle. Earlier in this book I discussed the concept that everything co-existed in a unified energy field and 'Ki, 'the underlying ingredient permeated and connected the Universe together; the inherent energy within everything being in constant resonance with everything else. From a singular perspective, the quality of our energy defines what we attract to ourselves and this is determined by the nature of our thoughts and intentions. An example of this is synchronistic phenomena, like the story of 'Dolly, the dead dishwasher'.

Through this book I have echoed the beliefs of early Taoists, that we are one with everything, there is no separation and all is born from the primordial essence, the Yuang Qi. So the question arises, was Mikao Usui suggesting that through the development of 'correct thought' we could become aware of our energetic connection to everything else in the universe and mindful of our original nature? Was he encouraging us to look within, to find the essence of our being, pure consciousness?

As I ponder this, I can see how this symbol is wonderfully interrelated with the story of the previous two symbols we have discussed. It inspires us to develop an inner connection to universal flow and infers if we find it, awaken it, listen to it and allow it to inform us, the realisation can occur that we are all part of the great universal unfolding. It is highly probable that Mikao Usui's intention for Symbol 3, was to remind us that our 'original nature', 'the essence of our being' and 'the origin of all' is pure consciousness flowing through everything.

So if it is true and we are already connected to everything, calling it distant healing is somewhat misleading because in universal terms there really is no such thing as separation. The symbol is not there to help us connect to someone distant from us, instead it is there to remind us we are already connected. Distant healing is the realisation that everything is 'One' and what we send out into the world reflects the quality of our thoughts and intentions. Distant healing therefore stops being something that we send to a person or event apart from us and becomes something we do with the awareness that the person or event is part of us.

Through the use of this symbol, a Reiki practitioner begins to understand how thoughts and intentions shape not only their own life but also impact on the people and environment around them. It is a call to become aware, mindful and responsible for what we are projecting into the world and to ensure we do our absolute best to emit positive loving energy.

Everyone on this planet is a master of manifestation and when we become the shepherd to our thoughts, and ensure that they are loving and positive, the world appears to greet us with love and positivity. Things seem to flow more readily as if we are in a state of grace. Even when things appear to block our path, we can view them as part of the flow, slight diversions designed to slow us a little. We can use them to regroup and course correct rather than continue to exercise our will and become frustrated.

Intention is a powerful tool and with practice, we can begin to see how effective we are at attracting things into our lives. Once I was driving some friends to a restaurant in Lake Como in the north of Italy and as I arrived near the restaurant it was absolutely packed and one of them said;

"You will never find anywhere to park around here".

"Its all about timing" I replied and with that, a car pulled out right in front of us leaving a space for us to park!

As superficial as manifesting a parking space may seem, the process of getting one regularly, is a wonderful illustration of these principles at work.

"THEN LAST OF ALL, HE SAW THE
GREAT WHITE LIGHT COMING."

HAWAYO TAKATA

SYMBOL 4.

THE MASTER SYMBOL

MANTRA – DAI KO MYO (DKM)

DAI – GREAT, KO – LIGHT, MYO – SUN AND MOON TOGETHER
MEANING BRIGHT

TRANSLATION, "THE GREAT BRIGHT LIGHT" OR
"THE GREAT SHINING LIGHT"

Our journey through the Reiki symbols ends with symbol 4. Its mantra is Dai Ko Myo [DKM]. Symbol 4 is known as the master symbol and is composed of a series of kanji characters combined together to form a pictograph but unlike Symbol 3, the characters are not compressed together. The symbol and its mantra therefore read the same. The Kanji that form this symbol are also found in Chinese where they read as Daguangming pronounced 'Dahgwahng ming.' In China Daguangming is commonly seen in shopping centres, arcades, cinemas in signage. It is also used to mark temples and there is a bridge over the Haihe river called Daguangming.

Because of the common existence of the kanji in symbol 4, there are those who have suggested it was never part of the Reiki system taught by Chujiro Hayashi. This is puzzling because we know symbol 4 is part of the system that Hawayo Takata learnt from Chujiro Hayashi. As I have great faith in both their teachings, let us explore the background to symbol 4 and see what we can uncover about its inherent value.

We can translate the mantra DKM to mean;

Dai – Great   Ko - Light   Myo - Bright

It has therefore been suggested that DKM represents 'enlightenment'.

We receive this symbol when we make the choice to become Reiki masters. So it is worth looking at what that title means in order for us to get a better idea why symbol 4 is included in the Reiki system. Like distant healing the title 'Reiki Master' is misleading, for it suggests we have become a master of Reiki. But with everything we have learnt about Reiki, it is clear that it is not something we can be master of. For it is the energy of Reiki that is our teacher and when we get out of its way and allow it to flow, it informs and directs our lives in every way.

So we might say, becoming a Reiki master is an indication that we have surrendered sufficiently to allow Reiki to flow spontaneously through most areas of our lives. We receive the master symbol in recognition that we have reached a sufficient level of maturity and it is at this point of our journey where others will turn to us for guidance.

Hawayo Takata taught the sole use of this symbol was to pass initiations where the master awakens the Reiki ability in a student, a kind of stirring of the seed of potential. If we follow that analogy and view each student as having a tree of knowledge lying latent within that seed, could symbol 4 be seen as the essential element required to stir that seed into life, the 'Great Bright Light'?

As the shepherd boy discovered in Paolo Coelho's Alchemist, the treasure that he dreamt of and travelled to the great pyramids to find, was buried beneath the tree under which he had slept the whole time. So is the treasure we seek hidden under our own figurative tree of knowledge, contained within the seed of our own potentiality? If so, it makes sense that the symbol that represents the 'Great Bright Light' is given to a master in recognition that their own journey has reached a satisfactory conclusion! For that reason, maybe a Reiki master can be viewed as the instrument through which the 'Great Bright Light' shines to encourage the seed in others to germinate and blossom?

So lets look into the mythology behind this symbol. A very compelling argument is that DKM is linked with Dainichi Nyorai, 'The Cosmic Buddha', 'The Great Illuminating One'. Dainichi Nyorai is also known as the Mahâvairocana Buddha or "Great Sun Buddha Of Light and Truth" and is likened to the sun that shines into every corner of the world dispelling darkness. The Great Bright Light, showing all living beings the way to 'enlightenment'. Dainichi is often portrayed with his hands in the six elements Mudra known as 'The Seal Of The Wisdom Fist' or 'Chiken-in-Mudra'. It symbolises the interpenetration of the two realms, Heaven and Earth and the perfection that can be found in union with the 'Great Bright Light' and 'Pure Consciousness' of God.

The elements of earth, water, fire, air and space represented by Dainichi's right hand grasping the upward pointing index finger of his left hand representing consciousness. The missing element of light is represented by Dainichi himself, being 'The Great Illuminating One". This Mudra, albeit not a part of the Reiki system itself, potentially offers us another piece to a very fascinating puzzle.

This reference to illumination and light is found in the story Hawayo Takata told of Mikao Usui;

"And he took a torch and walked up and down the mall where there were thousands of people" in the middle of the day. When he was told that he didn't need the torchlight, Usui said, "Yes, that is very true. But, I am looking and searching for people that have very sad, depressed minds. People who are unhappy. I am searching for people that need this light to brighten their hearts and cleanse their character and their mind and body."

We also find a continuance of the idea that to achieve 'enlightenment', we have to free the mind of its worry and confusion in a nine syllable Buddhist mantra which Dai Ko Myo happens to be a part of. It is called "Shiken Haramitsu Daikomyo".

SHIKEN

"The four hearts", represents four perspectives:

The Merciful Heart: expresses love for everything.

The Sincere Heart: follows what is right.

The Attuned Heart: follows the natural order of things.

The Dedicated Heart: holds to the chosen pursuit.

HARAMITSU

Is the Japanese pronunciation of the Sanskrit word Paramita which means that to reach enlightenment we have to free our minds from it's waves of worry, confusion and clutter.

DAIKOMYO

"The Great Shining Light" or "Great Enlightenment". Both the light that illuminates and awakens our own mind and the shining light that reveals the path to wisdom and understanding.

Hawayo Takata also related the story of Mikao Usui in the Buddhist Monasteries talking to a monk about physical healing. *"The monk said to him, Prayer in our chanting of the Sutras are very necessary in our faith and someday, during our various meditations, we shall receive that 'great light' and then we shall know."*

The concept of 'Enlightenment' is not exclusive to Buddhism however. If we can open our minds for a moment, take an anthropological shovel and dig into ancient Sumerian mythology, we find an interesting story of creation that echoes through history.

The Sumerian God of Sun and Sky was known as "An" His name means 'The Shining One'. The seven great angels "The Suns of the Shining One" or "Suns of Light" were called "Anunnaki ". They created the heavenly garden (E-din) on earth. For Sumerians E-din was the "abode of rightful ones" and it refers to an Aramaic root word meaning 'well watered and fruitful.' The tree of knowledge in the heavenly garden of E-din alluded to the secrets of the Shining One. This "tree" can be associated to the seven Chakras. The seed of our potential is akin to the coiled serpent at the base of the spine that rises up as Kundalini, ascending the Chakras to the crown where the wisdom of the journey is yielded. In Chakra theory, this is symbolised by two outstretched 'wings'.

"In the Sumerian "Black Book," Tawsi Melek 'The Peacock King' took 'Adam' the first human and transmitted the 'breath of life' into him. When Adam rose to his feet, Tawsi Melek quickly swung him around to face the Sun and told him that there was something much greater than he and that if Adam was righteous and true, one day he would know the supreme God who shone like the sun!

So we find a recurring concept through the migration and evolution of various psycho- spiritual ideas. Is it possible that encoded in Reiki there is a similar story? Mankind's potential to evolve from his earthbound nature, to refine and awaken his mind to become enlightened being represented by the Reiki symbols?

If true, it is not only hugely liberating but enables us to see the mirroring of archetypes through the various religious disciplines as they have migrated and evolved throughout the world. Is it possible Mikao Usui included them in the system of Reiki to tell us the story of our own essential nature? Together, the symbols reminding us to shine the 'Great Bright Light' on our shadows and reveal the hidden treasure within?

It was 'The Peacock King' who told Adam in the garden of E-din that one day he would know the supreme God who shone like the sun! Is the revelation contained within the Reiki symbols that once the seed within us germinates we are led to acknowledge ourselves as the snake? That by shining light into the shadows of our lives, we allow the snake to rise up from its earthly realm transforming snake venom and gaining a higher perspective? As we ascend the tree of knowledge and realise our greater purpose, do we metaphorically transform into the peacock with its shimmering tail feathers? Like Adam, are we to know the supreme God who shone like the sun? Can we like the 'mystical phoenix' embody the solar irridescence of the 'Great Sun Buddha'?

When Hawayo Takata told the story of Mikao Usui discovering Reiki she said,

"Then last of all, he saw the great white light coming from the right, and then like a screen they just stood right in front of him, like a screen. And when he drew his eyes to the screen, he saw what he had studied in the Sanskrit, one by one flew out, and then in golden letters, they just radiated out in front of him as if to say, "Remember! Remember!"

"I BELIEVE THERE EXISTS ONE SUPREME BEING
- THE ABSOLUTE INFINITE -
A DYNAMIC FORCE THAT GOVERNS
THE WORLD AND UNIVERSE.
IT IS AN UNSEEN SPIRITUAL POWER
THAT VIBRATES AND ALL OTHER POWERS
FADE INTO INSIGNIFICANCE BESIDE IT.
SO THEREFORE, IT IS ABSOLUTE.
THIS POWER IS UNFATHOMABLE, IMMEASURABLE
AND BEING A UNIVERSAL LIFE FORCE,
IT IS INCOMPREHENSIBLE TO MAN.
YET, EVERY SINGLE LIVING BEING
IS RECEIVING ITS BLESSINGS DAILY, AWAKE OR ASLEEP.
DIFFERENT TEACHERS AND MASTERS
CALL HIM THE GREAT SPIRIT,
THE UNIVERSAL LIFE FORCE, LIFE ENERGY,
BECAUSE WHEN APPLIED IT VITALISES THE WHOLE SYSTEM.
I SHALL CALL IT "REIKI"
BECAUSE I STUDIED UNDER THAT EXPRESSION."

HAWAYO TAKATA

PART 4.

THE REIKI PRACTICE

REIKI 1ST LEVEL

Reiki is the sacred energy of the universe that sustains all life.

A philosophy and system for personal development

A way to develop intuitive sensitivity

A powerful tool for navigation in life

A way to develop spiritual and self awareness

A powerful system that can be applied through touch and intent

The three realms, heaven earth and man, as a theme are echoed throughout Mikao Usui's system. Some say he was influenced greatly by the Taoist model of creation and when we move into the practice of Reiki perhaps it is fitting that it is learned in three levels.

In Part 1 we learned through our studies that the ancient pictograph of Ling Chi and Reiki represented the soul energy and tells the story of the methods that were evolved to deepen our relationship to this spiritual energy. The term Reiki is used to represent the systems practiced today that enable us to connect to this spiritual energy. In spite of the various claims of the many to be the sole keepers of Usui's original teachings, it is clear that over time many additions have been made. This is in part due to the migration of Reiki around the world and a natural consequence of the system evolving over the years.

Suffice it to say, from its humble beginnings Reiki has thrived. I trust in its intelligent flow and believe its success is down to its own desire being satisfied and can only be viewed as a reflection of its own inherent yearning to reach out and heal. As a community I hope we can look forward and allow Reiki to inform us how to refine practices, whilst retaining a respectful relationship to the pioneers of the past. If we are to truly honour Mikao Usui then let's cultivate his intuitive approach and allow Reiki to show us the way.

The credit must go to Hawayo Takata for the worldwide success of Reiki. She was the first master to teach outside Japan and the first to teach western people. In a recording of her made in 1979 when she was 78 years of age, she said,

"My students and my followers, learned this art of healing as the Usui Reiki Ryoho and in English, it is The Usui System in the Art of Healing. Reiki is a Japanese word, but in English it is Universal Life Energy. But I use it as Reiki because I learned in Japan, and therefore I still continue to say it in the short word Reiki".

She went on to say about Reiki that it was *"Gods plan. He gave us hands to use them to apply and heal, to retain physical health and mental balance, to free ourselves from ignorance and live in an enlightened world to live in harmony with yourself and others, to love all beings."*

Until 1982 Reiki, was an oral tradition, teachings being passed from master to student verbally. The emphasis placed on experiencing the practice by observing and replicating the teacher's methods until the student felt informed by the flow of Reiki themselves. Once that happened, it was considered the student was being taught by flow. Being guided by the energy is considered one of the essential elements required for a successful treatment. The development of intuition is part of the unfolding awareness within us when we connect to Reiki. Like a river cannot be pushed, guidance cannot be forced. It is achieved by remaining empty and present to what is. The most important thing about guidance is to remember it comes as a result of our alignment to flow, and our intention to go with it.

The journey begins when people make the choice to discover more about Reiki. Ironically, that is usually as a result of finally heeding the intuitive promptings and seeing the signposts that are urging us to take the first step. I remember my own journey to Reiki being littered with signs along the way trying to get my attention. In the end the recruitment team had to make it more obvious and literally tell me to do it. I am always intrigued to hear the stories of people who have chosen to train in Reiki. What made them decide, what steered them to come on that particular training course on that particular weekend? I always ask people to share their stories about how they arrived at my doorstep. The tales they tell are always filled with synchronistic events, chance encounters and improbable signs that they couldn't ignore. I see it as part of Reiki's flow, its longing for itself, reaching out for people to express itself through.

Richard Ellis

REIKI CIRCLE

"Being a universal force from the great Divine spirit, it belongs to all who seek and desire to learn the art of healing. It knows no color, nor creed, old or young. It will find its way when the student is ready to accept. He is shown the way"

Hawayo Takata

The journey often begins as a group of strangers in a room wondering what they have let themselves in for. The Reiki circle is an anchoring, settling meditation practice designed to harmonise all the different energies of the people into a united group. The Reiki teacher understands that energy flows according to its polarity and the left side of the body is associated to Yin [Feminine] and the right side of the body to Yang [Masculine]. Each member of the group is instructed to place their left palm facing upwards in front of them and place their right hand palm down on top. Then by simply opening the arms out to the sides they will find an upturned palm to their right and a downturned palm to their left to connect with. Some teachers will ensure a small space is left between the joining palms, so the flow of energy can be felt, others, encourage physical connection. The energy then naturally flows anticlockwise from left [Yin] to right [Yang] around the circle building in intensity the longer the group maintains the meditation. This is a powerful opening experience for many people due to the energy running around the circle and the sense of support felt by connecting to a group in this intimate way.

I use the Reiki circle in all of my group sessions and find, in a relatively brief amount of time, apparent strangers are prepared to open up and share. It's always interesting to see that the people gathered together have similar issues reflected in one another. It's as if they have been organised to attend the same workshop by an unseen hand, to best help and further their own personal development. As a variation to this exercise, the hands can be reversed allowing for a flow of energy in the clockwise direction. It is an interesting group activity to notice what occurs depending on the different direction of energy flow.

"Through the initiation we come to the
wonderfully simple realisation that
we are part of the great universal unfolding"

INITIATION

"Initiation is a sacred ceremony and the contact is made because we are associating with the Divine spirit. There is no error, nor should we doubt. It is absolute! With the first contact or initiation, the hands radiate vibrations when applied to the ailing part."

Hawayo Takata

The initiations represent the gift that is given to connect a student to the Reiki phenomenon. There is a sense of coming home, an awakening or a profound feeling of peace in this process. It varies depending on the individual and no two initiations are alike, some experience a gradual awakening, others are surprised at the power shaking them from their deep slumber. Many people report seeing the world as if for the first time, like it is in technicolour.

The Reiki initiation is an inherent part of our Reiki training. Many believe it forms a fundamental connection back to Mikao Usui himself. Each master in the lineage serving as a link in an energetic chain; without it, we cannot consider ourselves to be practicing authentic Usui Reiki Ryoho. Typically this has led to claims that some lineages have more pedigree than others. As Reiki expands throughout the world, and a growing number of lineages and systems appear out of the woodwork, confusion abounds.

In the west we use the words, initiation, empowerment and sometimes attunement to describe the ritual of transmitting Reiki. In Japan the word Reiju is used.

REI – We know describes, in essence, spirit. JU – means to grant.

The Initiation ritual taught by Hawayo Takata involves placing the Reiki symbols and mantras into key points in the students energy system to activate energy flow. The initiation can be viewed as a means of connecting the student to Heaven and Earth. The students microcosmic energy system, connected to the wider macrocosm.

I have been fortunate to facilitate many of these sacred ceremonies and seen the radical shift that occurs in a person. Not just in their ability to transmit healing energy but also in their state of being. The initiation appears to provide the impetus for a shift in perspective and reveals in a very real sense our true nature. Its as if the seed of our potential germinates in that very moment and we are given a glimpse of what we could grow into.

If I were to use one word to describe the feeling of passing an initiation to another, I would use the word, humbling! For it is in the passing of the initiation, that I experience the true grace inherent in the practice of Reiki. In that moment, there is a spontaneous alignment that takes place and I am aware of myself as a medium standing between Heaven and Earth. The ritual becomes something the Master and the student share and it feels profoundly sacred.

In Usui Reiki Ryoho, initiations are given to support the teachings at each level of the training. The two go hand in hand and you cannot have the training without the initiation ceremony or vice versa. Reiki is a spiritually guided system of healing for personal spiritual development and the ceremony provides the 'Rei', the spirit connection, that is essential to fully grasp the Reiki practice. So the teachings are given to us as concepts and practices that reveal how we can develop the connection we experience in the initiation ceremony. This is the path and if we follow it and utilise all the wisdom of the teachings, it could lead us to one day being the facilitator of the ceremony itself.

Despite this concept, the initiations in Reiki do not divide the levels in themselves and have nothing to do with the amount of energy or power a practitioner can channel. The levels simply divide the information and knowledge into sections that are being taught. The raising of awareness and the ability to feel and intuit energy flow is not guaranteed by simply receiving the initiation of that level. It is the continued practice of the contents of each level that determines our relationship to Reiki not just the initiation. People misunderstand this and it is perhaps unfortunate that so many relinquish personal responsibility and seek out teachers offering higher levels of Initiation beyond what is in the Usui Reiki Ryoho.

We are not required to elevate ourselves to connect to spirit, we do not need to leave the planet to become more divine. The suggestion that higher levels of awareness and spiritual vibration are available beyond Reiki is simply a gross misunderstanding of what Reiki is. We must remember that Reiki is about embracing emptiness. We need only surrender and let Reiki be our teacher. Let go of everything that inhibits connection and flow. Allow the love of spirit to infill us and diligently clear an empty space for it to dwell. The beauty is, the more we allow it in, the more we are informed by its flow and the more our lives are touched by its grace. This way our vibration is raised to a higher spiritual level entirely naturally as we are elevated by love.

I like to view the initiation as stirring the golden seed of potential within someone, that through gentle nurturing this seed can be allowed to grow and fill the space previously occupied by the old 'them'. Using this metaphor, we can see the importance of taking personal responsibility for the journey, utilising the tools given to us and making those changes that allow the seed to develop and flourish. When we do, we come to the wonderfully simple realisation that we are part of the great unfolding in this universe and we can relax into its warm embrace.

It has been suggested that Mikao Usui performed Reiju whenever he met with his students and that the Reiju was less structured than the sequence we use in the Usui Reiki Ryoho today. Exactly when those changes took place is unclear. It has also been suggested that students received Reiju simply by sitting with Mikao Usui and bathing in the energy that he transmitted. Some have implied that he was, at that moment, the embodiment of the deity Dainichi Nyorai, [the great shining light] allowing the emanation of that deity to transmit the Reiki energy to his students through him. If these reports are true, they would indicate that the Reiju was seen more as a kind of Darśana. This is a Sanskrit term meaning "sight" in the sense of gaining new awareness. It is commonly used in Hindu worship in reference to visions of the divine. One can also receive Darśana from a spiritual guru or master. A method used to cultivate spiritual awareness by transmitting the power of a Deity in this case Dainichi Nyorai.

This approach echoes many Vajrayana schools of Buddhism. Kobodaishi also known as Kukai was a tantric master who introduced the Vajrayana teachings in Japan in the early 9th Century and went on to establish the Shingon school of Buddhism. Kobodaishi established the Shingon temple on the sacred mountain Koyasan. Central to his philosophy was the notion that initiation formed a bridge between the Cosmic Buddha [Dainichi Nyorai] and the devotee. In the moment of initiation, the devotee is fully penetrated by the power of the Cosmic Buddha. Initiation is therefore seen, not only as a bridge to enlightenment, but also as a vehicle to unlock miraculous powers.

Kobodaishi taught that healing both the body and spirit was the first aspiration towards enlightenment. He said *"If practitioners do not go seeking for the remedies of the King of medicine, when will they ever be able to see the Light of the Great Sun."* There is certainly a compelling argument that Mikao Usui was utilising a similar approach to initiations however I cannot at this time validate it.

DISTANT INITIATIONS

With the growing trend in Internet training, there are many Reiki courses cropping up all over the Web with the bulk of the training given as correspondence and the initiation given from a distance. Proponents of these courses cite convenience and cost as the main incentives to study this way. Firstly, being able to fit your Reiki course into your busy life, studying when you want to and receiving the attunements in the quiet of your own home are certainly good arguments for this method of training. Secondly, the cost of remote courses is generally lower than the more traditional weekend format where your teacher is present. Advocates express the view that if it is possible to send healing at a distance then why limit ourselves to that and why not also send initiations? It is worth remembering that in Vajrayana Buddhism, the teachings only occur as direct transmissions from master to student through initiation and cannot be simply learned from a book.

Reiki is more than a system of healing to administer to others. It is a system designed for personal spiritual development. Through Reiki we can transform un-resourceful thought processes, clear blocked emotions and create balanced energy flow throughout our body. It is holistic and inclusive. The practice is there for our own self healing, helping us to change habitual behaviour, shift our perceptions, retrieve fragmented aspects of ourselves and reveal glimpses of our essential nature. It is very difficult to achieve this alone, as we have too many self-serving biases and blind spots. To embark on this journey without a teacher and only a handbook downloaded from the internet, is quite an undertaking. Having someone to steer us through a process enables us to bring our attention to aspects of our experience that we may not be paying attention to. I have come to the conclusion from the people I have encountered that anyone embarking on the Reiki journey who is tempted by distant courses will end up with more questions than answers and will very likely have to reinvest in further training in order to feel confident and proficient with the practice.

"To effectively assist the student to awaken to Reiki, the teacher needs to be present, needs to be able to watch for the physiological signs that the process is actually unfolding; to receive tangible energetic feedback. It would be disrespectful to the student to merely raise the hands at a distance, take the money and hope."

Kenji Hamamoto founder of Hekikuu Reiki

THE PRESENT IS LITERALLY THE GIFT OF THE NOW

"The creative act is an intense experience of the present, and as such, timeless."

Lama Govinda, The Foundations of Tibetan Mysticism

I remember when I was in my twenties and starting out on my personal journey of self discovery, I met an ex Pan Am Captain who had a wrist watch with the words NOW repeated all around the face of the watch in place of the numbers. It was a great reminder of the importance of staying present with what is.

All Eastern philosophies related to the gathering and utilisations of Ki have one essential element at the core of their teachings. The accessibility of the vital essence of life requires that we be in the present moment in order to notice it is there. The present moment is the place where we reconnect to our essential nature and, by virtue, reconnect to flow. In order to experience Ki, we have to shift our focus away from the external distractions and dramas of everyday life and realign ourselves within. To our surprise when we do, it takes very little to achieve deep connection inside, but the nature of the beast, is such, that we find life's dramas exact a strong pull on us and discipline is required to remain present.

With all the potential dramas occurring around us on a daily basis, it is no wonder we lose touch with the NOW. Feeling out of sync or in a bad place is generally a result of feeling disconnected from the flow of vital essence. Generally the reason people feel that way, is because they are placing their mind and thoughts somewhere else. In order to recognise flow we have to be still enough to feel its movement. Encouraging somebody to come back into the NOW to take advantage of the flow that exists there provides the opportunity to reconnect and be energised again.

As if by magic, people immediately start to feel whole again and discover a renewed sense of optimism. A good friend of mine's favourite saying was "Get your ducks lined up". Because when ducks aren't lined up, they are all swimming this way and that, quacking, going around in circles and causing chaos. Getting our own ducks lined up requires us to bring our minds back to the present, find our centre and reconnect to the flow once more. If not, we have to endure the drama of being pulled this way and that, expending loads of energy and achieving very little. When we do finally get back into the flow, we can see how out of sync we have been. Being in the flow is efficiency in action because we are aligned to universal grace. Things work out because we are where we are supposed to be!

The first step to shifting perception is to become orientated from within. Letting go of external distractions and interferences is part of our inner refinement and alignment to flow, which involves encountering stillness. To do that, we have to unplug ourselves from the social matrix, switch off the transmissions and distractions that have been designed to occupy us. As we take time to mindfully experience ourselves and just be, we create the space to settle within and reconnect to flow again. Flow informs us of choices we need to make, which naturally alter the way we feel and think about ourselves.

As we refine we become more aware of the destructive elements in our surroundings. We begin to notice where our inner and outer worlds lack congruency. As we tune in, we begin to recognise the need to make more resourceful and loving lifestyle choices. Suddenly old patterns of behaviour are no longer appropriate to what we are becoming. Adjustments in our routines are inevitable and we may find we drop aspects of our old self. Smoking, drinking alcohol, the foods we eat, the programmes we watch on TV, social media, negative thinking, conflicts, bad company, too much stimuli etc.. It all comes up for review so we can decide what stays and what goes and what supports the refinement taking place within.

Ultimately, a natural balance occurs between the progress on the inside through the meditations and practices used to cultivate Ki and the change on the outside through lifestyle choices and environments we choose to put ourselves in. As we begin to listen to this inner flow and allow it to inform us, there is a natural alignment between our inner and outer worlds that reflects those choices we make. To be cheerfully Chi full, we have to turn to life sustaining behaviours. In other words, to be Chi full requires us to live a life that fosters Chi.

The next step in our adventure is to connect mindfully with something that can act as an anchor to the NOW. In this way it is my aim to enable you, the reader, to cultivate a relationship to an inner flow. The process of learning and the process of development can then be prompted from within. The most suitable anchor is our breath. Like a restless tide it reminds us of our connection to the ocean of Ki and supports the gathering and expression of Ki in our body. I am going to share with you some mindful exercises utilising your breath. The following exercise will offer an opportunity to allow the natural forces around you to support the letting go of feelings and thoughts you may no longer wish to carry.

EXERCISE

Simple Lying down meditation- letting go

Lie on your back on the ground with your head supported by a small pillow, place the palms of your hands to the earth.

As you lay here relaxed, breathing easy and supported by the earth, notice what comes to mind, notice how you feel, be aware of areas that require unwinding.

Bring your awareness to your breath, as you breathe in and out, naturally be aware of your breath, touching your diaphragm.

Notice what feelings and sensations arise

Your breath is like an anchor… an anchor into the now, and in between your breaths you can explore the pause, the space…. each pause represents a decision to continue into the next now moment.

The now is where your mind and body can reconnect. Bring the mind home, and notice what needs letting go. Feel the force of gravity acting on the full surface of your body. Allow the force of gravity to draw what you no longer need into the earth beneath you. Let emotions, stresses, physical discomfort and thoughts go into the earth.

Allow your mind and body to be in a state of complete stillness. As you lay there you can bring your attention again to your breath. Notice if your diaphragm is more relaxed, allow your breath to penetrate deeper down into your abdomen, feel the rise and fall of your belly as you breathe.

With each breath, imagine that the whole surface of your body is breathing and you are drawing life giving energy into your lower belly.

To end, place the palms of your hands on your belly and notice what you notice.

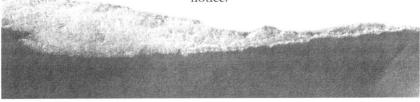

BEING MINDFUL

"The miracle of love comes to you in the presence of the un-interpreted moment. If you are mentally somewhere else, you miss real life."

Byron Katie

Just like Chi has become integrated into popular culture, so too has mindfulness. As concepts, the two are inseparably intertwined. Mindfulness means to pay precise, non-judgmental attention to aspects of our experience as they arise. Instead of struggling to get away from experiences we find difficult, we practice being with them. This works with pleasant experiences as well because we often have just as much of a hard time staying present with happiness as we do anything else, like worrying that it won't last or trying to keep it from fading away.

When a client comes to see me to discuss their problems, they are nearly always a result of the inner cognitions. Thoughts have an incredible capacity to arise out of nowhere and love nothing better than to distract us from the present moment. The mind is as adept at filling in details of various future scenarios as it is wallowing and reliving trauma from the past. The physical body meanwhile is stuck in the present and having to experience whatever the mind is focused on, as if it were actually there. An undisciplined mind will generally wander down well-trodden habitual pathways that re-enforce negative-patterned behaviour.

The remedy I have offered is not complicated, quite the opposite, It is to simply show people how to become mindful of the NOW. It is the natural antidote for nearly every ailment I have encountered. I can dress it up in many ways, I can give it different names and I can teach many methods to find it and yet still when all is said and done, it is within the simplicity of the NOW moment that healing occurs.

Aside from being an essential aspect of living with Reiki and giving a Reiki treatment, mindfulness extends to every waking moment of your life. Becoming mindful is to notice what is being presented. Incorporating mindful meditation as part of your daily Reiki practice is a great way to settle within and bring awareness to what presently is happening. It is called the 'present' moment because it is where the gifts of our lives are to be found. When we are mindful, we literally choose to show up in our lives.

So, how do we actually practice mindfulness meditation? There are four aspects worked with in mindfulness: Our body, breath, thoughts and focus. In order to bring the mind home we require something to focus upon that is fully present. Fortunately our bodies offer us an anchor and are a great place to start, because they cannot escape the NOW.

MINDFUL MEDITATION

A Mindful Meditation

STAGE 1. BODY - Be in a relaxed sitting position where you will be able to close your eyes and rest without being disturbed. Before you close your eyes, get a sense of your body and a sense of where you are. Be aware of what you are sitting or lying on, the support, the texture, the comfort, the temperature. Notice what you can see, the direction you are looking, the quality of light, notice what you notice. Focus on the sensations in your body as you interact with your environment, the movement of each breath, the temperature of the air you are breathing in and out, the sound of breathing, your heart beating, your feet down there on the floor, your hands resting there. Feel your feet on the floor. Close your eyes and explore what it is like to be inside yourself. Compare being inside to being outside. Open your eyes for a moment before closing them again.

STAGE 2. BREATH - Rest your attention lightly on the breath. There's no special way to breathe in this technique. We are interested in how we already are. If you find that you are controlling your breath, just let it be, however it is. Notice what emotions and feelings in your diaphragm are associated to the way you are breathing. What happens when you notice them? What does it feel like to touch those emotions with your breath?

STAGE 3. THOUGHTS - As you sit practicing, you will notice what kinds of thoughts are occurring. Sometimes there are a great many thoughts overlapping with no apparent significance or origin. Other times they may be specific and elicit strong emotions and are hard to let go of. If you notice that you are so caught up in thoughts that you have forgotten that you're sitting in the room, you can mentally say "I was thinking" and gently bring yourself back to your breath. Remember that mindfulness meditation is about practicing being mindful of whatever happens. It is NOT about trying to stop ourselves thinking.

STAGE 4. FOCUS - Finally, direct your breath to your lower abdomen. Focus all your attention on your Hara. Stay relaxed and observant as you breath to this area. Notice the rise and fall of your belly and allow yourself to sink down deeply inside yourself. Notice the sensations that occur as you bring all of your awareness to this part of your body. Be aware of changes in temperature and flow within. Rest in your Hara.

PREPARATION

In many ways, simple intent is all that is required to create energy flow if one is grounded, open and present. Many of the techniques designed to open up the central channel and create flow are tools to bring us into the Now. The simplest way of doing this is to drop into our body by focusing on our breath and the Hara. This relaxes both body and mind. Bringing our hands together in Gassho over our heart connects the laogong points in the palms of our hands and quite naturally creates flow. There are more involved ways to stimulate Reiki energy flow and these techniques are useful but it is worth remembering that Reiki is with us always. As Hawayo Takata taught, Reiki starts when you put your hands on someone and stops when you take your hands off. However, there are days when flow occurs more easily than others and this is a reflection of our present state of openness. These techniques therefore can help us on those days and are designed to re-centre and rebalance our system.

There are several elements to preparation that can be done as stand-alone practices or put together. They are dry brushing, purification meditation [visualising light filling the energy system] sometimes with some basic Qigong moves, Gassho Meditation and recital of the five principles. I would personally add invocation in the form of a prayer to this process, as I believe it is an important part of honouring ones lineage.

DRY BATHING

The forms of dry bathing being taught today are actually simplified Qigong clearing forms. For example the brushing of the arms is a standard clearing technique however in Qigong it is typically done using all four quadrants of the arm rather than just the upper quadrant taught in some systems.

The important thing to remember when doing dry bathing is that the movements follow actual meridian lines. Also, sometimes movements to the energy field can have more effect than actual physical brushing does.

On the next page is an unorthodox, non-traditional, effective dry bathing technique I wish to share with you.

A DRY BATHING TECHNIQUE

Stand feet shoulder width apart knees slightly bent

Breathe in through the nose and then brush your hands through your hair
from front to back and down your neck come round to the front over
your collar bones and sweep down either side of your chest into the earth
as you exhale quickly through your mouth.

Then brush the backs of your hands downwards past your kidneys (lower
back) vigorously towards the earth.

Breathe in again through your nose and exhale through your mouth

Brush down your left arm and off the fingers with your right hand
into the earth

Brush down your right arm and off the fingers with your left hand
into the earth

Brush diagonally with your right hand from your left shoulder
to your right hip

Brush diagonally with your left hand from your right shoulder
to your left hip

Finally, as you breathe in, gather energy upwards with your hands
[palms up] from below your pelvis through your whole body
following the central midline your hands rotate [palms up]
at your chest area and continue past your crown and up into the air.
They then separate and make a circular downward motion
through your external energy field until the finger tips
meet again below your pelvis. Repeat again three times.
(This will strengthen your energy system)

GASSHO MEDITATION

One of the first steps learnt in creating energy flow as a Reiki practitioner is the Gassho Meditation used to manifest vital energy for health and wellbeing and as a precursor to treating another person. Daily use of this meditation can increase your vitality and strengthen your disposition helping you to stay healthy in all seasons. As a practice, it represents a way to gather and replenish internal Ki in the Lower Dantian that then gets circulated throughout the reservoirs and channels of the energy system. The left hand [Yin] represents our human nature and the right [Yang] represents our spirit nature. Brought together over the heart or Middle Dantian they symbolise oneness, the integration of heaven and earth in physical form made possible through the loving power of the heart.

The Gassho meditation brings together the lower Dantian in the belly, the middle Dantian in the heart and the 'Lao Gong' or 'Palm chakras' in the hands. When breathing to the Lower Dantian is introduced, Ki "spreads like an enshrouding mist" between the Lower Dantian and the Middle Dantian. The Ki generated is often experienced as heat as it radiates out to the palms of the hands. The 'Lao Gong' or "Palm chakras", providing a destination for energy to flow to from the heart, actively stimulating greater flow and sensitivity in the palms.

On Page 203 I will be discussing the Gassho in more detail and describing how it can be used to set up intention.

Gassho

EXERCISE TO EXPERIENCE GASSHO MEDITATION

Sit quietly and place the hands in Gassho (Prayer Position) over the heart
and bring your attention to the breath.

Whist breathing in, be mindful of drawing energy in, through the full
surface of your body, from all around you to the
Lower Dantian in the Hara (Belly).

Whilst you breathe out focus on the energy generated in the
Lower Dantian and allow it to spread up through your body,
up to your Middle Dantian [heart].

As the flow of energy increases allow it to flow from the heart
down your arms to the Lao Gong in your hands.

Keep focusing and breathing on the Lower and Middle Dantians
until your whole body feels charged with Reiki
and your hands feel very hot.

Even on it's own, the Gassho Meditation is a powerful way
to prepare yourself for the phenomena of Reiki prior to
self healing or giving a treatment to another.

With practice and experience, energy can be directed outwards into the
space around you to create a field charged with Ki.

PURIFICATION MEDITATION

PURIFICATION MEDITATION

This is a purifying technique using visualisation and breath
to clear and strengthen your energy. There are several variations
that essentially follow the same route. This is the one I use.

Ensure you won't be disturbed and induce a relaxed state prior
to starting with self-meditation breathing into your Hara.

Sitting down on a chair hands on your lap, visualise a sphere
of white light above your head.

See it radiating a purifying and clearing light in all directions

See the sphere descend down through the crown radiating
purifying light in all directions clearing all blocked energy.

See the sphere descend through the centre line of your body,
clearing and purifying as it goes.
As it radiates light in all directions allow the sphere to descend
down to the Seika Tanden filling it with light
see the sphere expanding filling your whole body with light.

Continues to expand the sphere out into your energy field
filling your aura with light
Expand the sphere further out boundlessly to infinity

To end

Feel your feet on the floor hands on your lap
Be aware of your breath and the sensations of your body
In your own time when you're ready open up your eyes.

THE FIVE REIKI PRINCIPLES

The Five Reiki Principles are an important part of our Reiki training and continuing self-development. The five principles created by Mikao Usui as a set of precepts for his students were usually recited in Gassho Meditation. Hyakuten Inamoto of Komyo Reiki say's "The five precepts are based on a phrase in the opening page of a book "Kenzen no genri" or "The principle of soundness". Written by Dr. Suzuki Bizan and published on December 28, in the 3rd year of Taisho [1914].

The precepts are known in Japan as the Gokai and there are many English versions. Simply they say;

JUST FOR TODAY

DO NOT ANGER

DO NOT WORRY

BE GRATEFUL

WORK DILIGENTLY

BE KIND TO ALL LIVING THINGS

When we look at the principles we see there is a natural logic to them. Releasing anger and worry can only be done if we bring our mind home into the present moment. Gratitude is a natural by-product of being present in the now. We can begin to notice how many gifts there are in our life when we open our eyes to look for them. When we have a grateful heart, we can get on with our work diligently enjoying a sense of contribution to the whole. Kindness to others is natural when we realise how interconnected everything is and that also happens when we become mindful of the now. We cannot hope to be kind to others until we have released the anger and worry within ourselves and reside in a grateful heart that wishes to contribute to the greater good.

As a hypnotherapist I studied the efficacy of repetitive suggestions and I am very aware of the positive effects they can have. One of the rules of suggestion is that they are stated in the positive and progressively. The old adage is, If I say to you "Don't think of a blue elephant", you can't carry out the instruction without first having to imagine a blue elephant. In relation to the Five Reiki Principles, by suggesting, "Just for today do not worry", I am in effect asking you to focus on your worry. Due to this I have struggled over the years with the standard translations of the five precepts and it has motivated me to make them more progressive, which allows me to utilise them in the context of my daily life without losing sight of their essence.

JUST FOR TODAY

I RELEASE MY INVESTMENT
IN STAYING HURT AND ANGRY

I RELEASE WORRY AND STAY MINDFUL
OF THE PRESENT MOMENT

I AM GRATEFUL AND APPRECIATE THE WONDERS
AND BLESSINGS IN MY LIFE

I DO MY WORK DILIGENTLY AND WITH LOVE,
EVEN THE SMALLEST TASKS

I SHOW KINDNESS
TO ALL LIVING THINGS

HOLDING A SPACE FOR HEALING

"The highest virtue is to act without a sense of self
The highest kindness is to give without a condition
The highest justice is to see without a preference"

Verse from the Dao de Jing translated by Jonathan Star

Being completely surrendered and empty enables us to hold a space for Ki to flow into and actively stimulate whoever or whatever is within it. Healing is a spontaneous response to the resonance that has arisen in the situation and a healing space enables qualities of resonance to be heard more easily. Going into a sacred healing place has a profound impact on people. If they feel supported by an empathetic practitioner who is in tune with what is taking place, change happens effortlessly and there is no need for force.

There is an art to holding a space for another. It requests a great deal of concentration. We are required to listen, observe and surrender ourselves into an energetic relationship whilst not losing sight of who we are. We have to merge and experience the quality of the interaction, whilst reminding ourselves, it is not ours to carry once the healing is done. Holding a space requires us to be open and flexible and to let go of preconceived ideas of what is to take place whilst in the space. This allows an emerging of a healing process that is congruent with the needs of the person we are focusing on.

A client comes to receive. What they choose to take from the experience will be down to them. Our clients don't need to know about our needs, our expertise, our opinions, our projections or our insecurities. As soon as we worry about the outcome, as practitioners, we have made it about us. That is contra to the flow and there are issues that can arise from doing this. We may start to try harder, or push more, thinking added energy is needed to achieve the outcome we want. This approach is destined to lead us to one destination…Depletion of our own energy reserves! The more we try, the more tired we will become. The more we push someone towards some desired outcome, the less congruent we are. The more we try to fix someone and send them home healed, the more we have robbed them of their own responsibility to heal themselves. When we invest something of ourselves in the outcome and when we make it about us, it is no longer about our client.

It takes practice to be able to step out of the way and remind ourselves all healing is self-healing. We want to help and make it better but have to learn to let Reiki reawaken the memory of being whole again. We don't know what that may involve or mean for someone. What steps are necessary for them to take, what needs to be processed or how much time is required.

I see healing like a story, there is a beginning, middle and an end. It begins quietly from a place of stillness. Then as the energy flows and informs movement, something arises from the interplay, like a dance. For a moment, it is as if awareness is elevated, senses heightened and veils are removed. Something shifts, is understood, realised and then all is quieted, returning once again to stillness.

Learning to put down the interaction and involvement with our client once it has passed comes with experience. The less we hold onto it, the more confidence we develop to be open and accessible the next time. It is important to learn that any feelings we encounter are transitory and we do not need to carry them into our own lives, beyond the treatment.

At this point, the issue of protection is often raised.

WILL I BE PROTECTED WHEN I GIVE REIKI?

"We cannot be more sensitive to pleasure without being more sensitive to pain".

Alan Watts

This is one of the most frequently asked questions in my Reiki classes and I will explain my own philosophy on the subject and the wider implications of holding onto the need for protection.

A quick search on Google reveals opposing views on the subject. One camp firmly believing in the need for some additional measures to be taken in order to feel protected from outside energies and there are many inventive methods listed that claim to offer this. "Aura Shields, Reiki Bubbles, Earth Bound Spirit Flush", are just a small sample of what is out there.

The other camp believes Reiki requires no other protection than what it naturally affords. Hawayo Takata apparently held this belief and is quoted to have said,

"Your Reiki power is like an aura, its a glow, and you are radiating out, and that energy is stronger than what can penetrate into you … no darkness can penetrate you"

A good place to begin is to look at what 'the need for protection' presupposes..

I am light and what I need protecting from is dark
I am positive and what I need protecting from is negative
I am good and what I need protecting from is evil
My personal boundaries need re enforcing
There are outside forces that can influence me negatively
Other people's energy can get stuck in me
Reiki alone is not powerful enough to protect me
Dark forces are powerful
I am not safe

Two things strike me about this list, firstly how clearly it reflects a fearful state of being and secondly a deep need to re-enforce personal boundaries.

In Chakra Theory we would narrow these two issues down to the psychological aspects of the base and sacral Chakras. The Base Chakra is where we develop a grounded and trusting relationship to the physical Universe. The sacral Chakra is where we develop a sense of personal value and learn to enforce healthy boundaries.

I am a great believer in the idea that the world is simply a reflection of our present projections upon it. Could it then be that the need to protect oneself from perceived external threats is simply a reflection of our own inner cognitions and beliefs? When we strip down and analyse the need for protection, we can begin to see it as something we feel the need to do inside our own minds in order to feel more comfortable with our external experience. Visualising a sphere of light around us, or a Reiki shield is done using the imagination within the mind after all.

Were we to realise that the way we experience the outside world the whole time, is a direct result of our present state of mind, wouldn't it just be simpler to change our way of thinking instead? Surely the more we focus on our discomfort with different spectrums of energy and emotion, the greater the need to protect ourselves from them? What if we challenged the belief that there was something 'out there' that we needed to protect ourselves from? Targeting the fundamental core belief that we are unsafe would mean that we could meet different energies that we encounter daily with curiosity and explore the way they make us feel without moving into fear of what they might do to us.

In my classes I say, 'the only thing you need protecting from is yourself'. This is because it is your own thoughts about a situation that defines your experience of it. If you hold the belief that something is dark, negative or evil, you will, I have no doubt, experience it as such. Before you know it, you'll be seeking help from other people holding a similar view and attempting to rid yourself of the 'entity' you have created in your own mind.

The ability of the human imagination to expand upon an idea seeded with fear is without question. Right through human history you will find examples of the struggle between dark and light that have contributed to this idea we are not safe. It is rooted deep inside our psyche and constantly re-enforced. Religions reflect these beliefs and without the allegiance and protection of said religion will result in your soul being lost for an eternity to the dark forces. These ideas have found their way into modern mainstream thinking almost as part of our collective inheritance. From fairytales to blockbuster movies like Star Wars, the theme is light overcoming dark. No wonder then that many practitioners have adopted the idea of a universe polarised by positive and negative forces and come up with creative ways to deal with the perceived threat.

I teach students to view everything they come into contact with as simply energy. Some of it feels nice and some not so nice. Our ability as healers to feel the sensations which guide us to the areas most in need, relies on us being able to merge energetically with our client.

Protection is only needed if a position is taken. Let me explain. When 'the you' and 'the me' meet to become 'the we' the resonance that occurs is a result of our interaction. Afterwards when 'the we' becomes 'the you' and 'the me' again, we cease to resonate unless either of us chooses to hold onto the interaction. People who need protection are holding onto 'the me' as they enter into the interaction of 'the we' and when the interaction is over holding onto 'the we' when they should be returning to 'the me'. Simple..

THE GOLDEN RULES ARE

Erecting a shield when you feel something unpleasant just serves to trap it within, stay open and you will be more able to let it go.

If you are mindful of your own energy prior to a treatment then any change during a treatment will be a result of the interaction with your client.

If you feel depleted after giving Reiki, it is because you have invested yourself in the outcome. Let Reiki flow and get out of the way.

View strong feelings that arise during a treatment as an indication of how present you are with your client in their process.

Know that you're safe and can release any unwanted feelings that have arisen during a treatment easily once your client has gone.

A USEFUL AFFIRMATION

"NO PERSON, PLACE OR THING CAN DISTURB MY SENSE
OF PEACE AND CALMNESS WITHIN."

GUIDANCE

"Be still and listen for guidance, stillness is the language God speaks and everything else is a bad translation."

Eckhart Tolle

When we allow ourselves to be inspired by spirit [inspirited] to do something, we are influenced by divine flow. Our thoughts and actions are guided to be appropriate for the given moment because we are present with what is. Our connection to internal Ki is rich with information. We become in that instant intuitively directed. Guidance is our ability to perceive subtle information. This arises during the interaction with our client and may affect and positively influence the outcome of the treatment. Our ability to sense this information when it presents itself is directly related to our ability to be empty.

Once we have established a connection to the internal flow of Ki we feel ourselves being replenished and can relax into the healing experience. At an energetic level, when we enter into a healing relationship with someone, it can feel boundary less. We realise that we are connected to the other as part of a whole. The connection is experienced as resonance and what takes place affects us together. It's important not to think of the other as someone else. Think of you both as 'us'. It is easier for 'us' to be lead by Ki than it is for 'me' to move 'you'.

Within this dynamic resonance, information appears as intuitive promptings, inner knowing's, images and sounds pertaining to the healing taking place. It's like a wireless network linking devices together being connected to an information superhighway.

Ted Kaptchuk writes; "This ability for one thing to influence another is called in Chinese 'gan ying', which is usually translated as "resonance". If qi is the link, resonance is the method.... Resonance is the process by which a thing when stimulated, spontaneously responds according to the vital energy engendered in itself and active in the situation."

The emptier we are, the greater the Ki flow. The greater the ki flow the higher the resonance. The higher the resonance, the greater the potential response. The more open we are to Ki flow the more communication can be present. The information is there within the Ki informing whoever is willing to listen. The interesting thing is that it is not just the healer that can interpret this information but also the client.

The person who is most effective at becoming empty and open is usually the one who is not trying. The Ki flow is interrupted by our own needs and wants. The more we are able to let go of conditions and preferences, the further Ki informs us. It's not easy for an ego to be deeply surrendered and not make things about itself. It's not easy to release outcomes and simply hold a space for someone else unconditionally. We like to feel useful, we like to think of ourselves as making a difference. We want to know that we have helped facilitate change. But all that just gets in the way and prevents us really being completely open and surrendered to what is. This takes us back to wu wei as a concept; [The efficiency of non-action] Rather than trying to force a result upon another, we must allow it to unfold naturally. Allow the flow to reveal what is required and guide us to the right outcome.

A LITTLE EXERCISE

Stand with your feet shoulder width apart;
relax your ankles, knees and pelvis.

Bring your awareness to your Hara
Breathe so your belly expands and contracts.

Begin to shake out your body from the Hara,
gently at first then more vigorously

Allow your whole body to shake and release

Then let the shaking decrease by half, then by half again, then by half,
half-half-half-half, until you are still vibrating but so subtly and
imperceptibly that on the inside you are perfectly still.

SCANNING

"Don't move the move, let the move, move you."

Stuart Shaw Tai Chi teacher

Our ability to tune into subtle energies is reliant on a slight shift in perception akin to tuning a radio receiver. The energy is always there regardless of whether someone can perceive it or not. Once tuned in, we can experience the many realms and vibrations. As we learn to listen and build a relationship to Ki, what previously was intangible becomes tangible and we learn to utilise it and be informed by its flow. The reason Ki remains outside of many people's experience is because it is so easy to get lost in the coarseness of existence that we cannot sense the subtleties.

Scanning

There are various methods employed to intuit the energetic landscape of a person to know what is required during a healing. The supposition being that if an illness exists; there will be an accompanying resonance [Hibiki] that an experienced Reiki practitioner can detect. This is an intuitive practice guided by the flow of Ki energy active in the situation. The Reiki practitioner allows themselves to be informed by this flow and is able to feel various sensations in the energetic field around a client. Usually these are experienced as changes in flow, temperature, pressure, vibration, intensity or weight. Some people report experiencing a feeling of being pulled or directed to areas, some actually feel the pain or discomfort in their own bodies and others say they just seem to know where to go. In other words, the practice of scanning is unique to each person and requires us to develop our own intuitive methodology.

With the experience I have had in teaching this method over the years, I have found people can fall at the first hurdle due to a simple fact; they wait to feel what is required in order to begin the healing. Instead my advice is always, start the healing and then feel what is required. Once we have started two things happen.

1. We move from a thinking state to a being state.

2. Energy begins to flow informing us of where to go and what's required.

So let's take a look step-by-step at the process of scanning.

- The trick is to begin slowly about 6 to 8 inches away from the recipient's body moving in an anticlockwise direction around them and through the full length of their body.

- Remember whatever you do, try not to think about it too much. Just cultivate curiosity and be intrigued by what happens.

- Don't try and log all of the problems and make mental notes of everything you feel. Instead remember it is an unfolding process and just look for a starting point.

- Once you've found somewhere to begin, just let energy flow and see where it takes you. Allow the energy to inform you of where it wants you to go next.

There can be a variety of experiences people have and for the most part it is positive, sometimes people don't feel very much at first and usually this is a result of them getting in the way of the process. Things that can prevent you feeling anything at all will normally fall under the following;

- Worrying about not being able to do it.

- Trying too hard.

- Over thinking things.

- Projecting onto your partner what you should be feeling based on what you know about them.

- Not relaxing enough.

There are also times when you can experience unpleasant feelings when doing this practice and these can include;

- Overwhelming emotion.

- Feeling sick or nauseous.

- Light-headedness.

- Feeling too hot, claustrophobic or overwhelmed.

- Feeling pain in your body or in your hands.

- Severe backache.

- Involuntary movement in your hands or body.

If you do feel overwhelmed or experience unpleasant feelings throughout this exercise, step away from the interaction, consciously ground yourself by focusing your breath on your Hara and see if the feelings pass. If not, have a break and get some fresh air. It is really important to begin to see the feelings that we have when giving Reiki as transitory. The more open we are, the more we feel and equally the more relaxed and open we are, the easier it is for us to let go afterwards.

I love observing students experiencing this on a Reiki 1st level course. No experience, no preconceived notions of what is and isn't possible and no comparisons taking place with each other yet. The result is always outstanding with students achieving incredible accuracy and empathy with the person they are working with. One particular lady that I was teaching, Sharon, had come to the course purely to learn how to do self-treatment for her own particular physical condition that she was struggling with at the time. She confessed to me after the training that prior to us doing this particular exercise she was ready to run away feeling completely out of place and out of her comfort zone. Her practice partner was lying down on a massage table and I invited Sharon to come and stand on the right hand side and instructed her how to begin. I made sure that she was rooted to the earth and began with some Gassho Meditation, ensuring she was connected to her internal Ki before she began.

Following my directions, she moved anticlockwise through her partner's energy field remaining very focused and silent. After two circuits her hands suddenly started to shake involuntarily and her expression changed to one of complete surprise. She looked up at me as if to say 'help what on earth is going on?' I reassured her and asked what she felt? Her hands at that moment were hovering over her partner's lower abdomen and shaking quite strongly. "I feel like there's a hole that needs filling up with love and energy" She replied. I suggested she continue giving energy to that particular area until she felt that it was time to move somewhere else or do something else. She remained there for a good 30 minutes during which time she continued to shake, got very hot and tears started to run down her face.

Afterwards the three of us had a chat and it turned out that in the area she was working, her partner's right kidney had been removed about 10 years beforehand due to cancer. What was incredible was Sharon's ability to not only feel the area that required energy but also her sense of the hole that was left behind by the organ being removed. The experience for Sharon was life changing and gave her an awareness of her own intuitive connection to Reiki. She has since gone on to become a Reiki Master in her own right.

There are some rules I have observed to energy flow and they are;

- Emotion is generally released upwards as expression, the block is invariably found at the solar plexus.

- The diaphragm will often be contracted in an effort to control emotions by keeping them suppressed.

- Release of emotion is often accompanied by deep abdominal breathing.

- Fear and toxicity is generally released downwards into the earth. The earth loves to compost our stuff.

CLEARING ENERGY

If it is true that whatever we focus our minds upon becomes our experience, it would follow that letting go of something requires us to first release our attention upon it. Much of our perception and the attachment we form to energies experienced through a treatment are a result of how we think about them. I have talked about people feeling the need to protect themselves from external energies and the elaborate ways they formulate to do this. Our perception of external energies begins within the mind and is based on our beliefs and internal representations. We therefore experience them depending upon our thoughts about them.

It is my experience that altering our thinking and internal cognitions rather than trying to control the external world is more effective. Far better to be empowered, choosing how we respond to energies we encounter, than reacting to external energies and constructing barriers to protect ourselves. It is as simple as deciding to come from love rather than fear.

Once we have allowed our mind to become more flexible it is remarkably easy to open ourselves to energies, merge with them, feel them and then let them go. Use the Dry Bathing and Purification Meditation both before and after treatments to help clear your energy.

FULL TREATMENT

Through the practice of scanning we will have realised our ability to intuit the energetic landscape of our clients. With confidence we can allow ourselves to be informed by flow to the areas that require healing. However in the early stages of treating others, it is helpful to have a format and sequence to follow. It should not take the place of working intuitively, and is there primarily to install confidence and as an aid to developing our spontaneous approach.

Like most approaches to Reiki, there are numerous instructions on hand position that have been developed through the different schools over the years. Most use a sequence travelling downwards from the head to the feet. If we think of ourselves as an empty vessel standing between Heaven and earth, it makes sense to follow the central channel and concentrate on the Chakra points. As practitioners we are looking to clear this central channel of restrictions, helping to reconnect our clients to the flow of energy coming from heaven and earth. These polarities find their own balance when flowing freely through the system.

Ordinarily restrictions are a result of carrying contractions throughout the energetic system. This will show up physically in the musculoskeletal systems and organs. They are also revealed in the general psychological and emotional demeanour of a person. With that in mind, the Reiki full treatment can be seen as a holistic approach where the emphasis is on de-stressing, harmonising and replenishing the energy of your client. Whenever possible, the whole system is treated and it is hoped, the symptoms regardless of what they are improve or disappear naturally.

The following are a suggested set of hand positions for you to use. Remember hand positions are there as a guide and do not need to take the place of your intuition. Feel free to follow the flow of each individual treatment you give and return to the hand positions when it feels natural to do so. Ideally a natural balance can be developed between structure and flow.

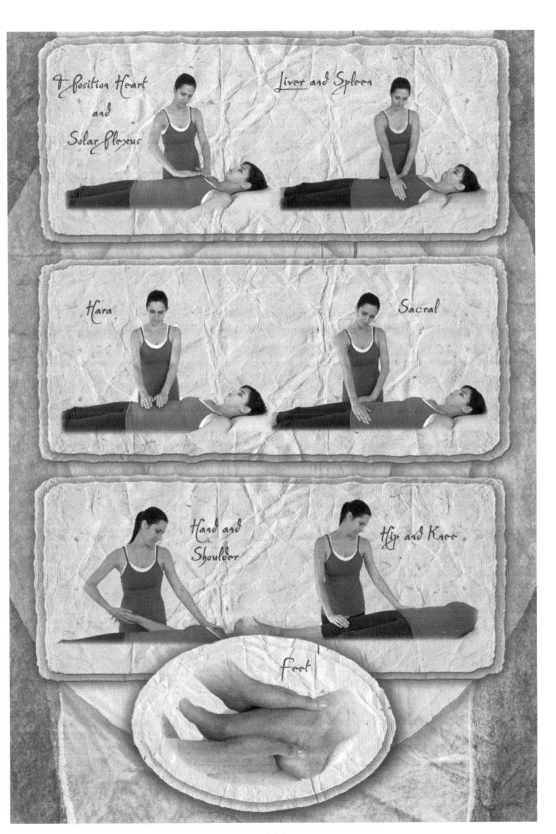

Position Heart and Solar Plexus

Liver and Spleen

Hara

Sacral

Hand and Shoulder

Hip and Knee

Feet

167

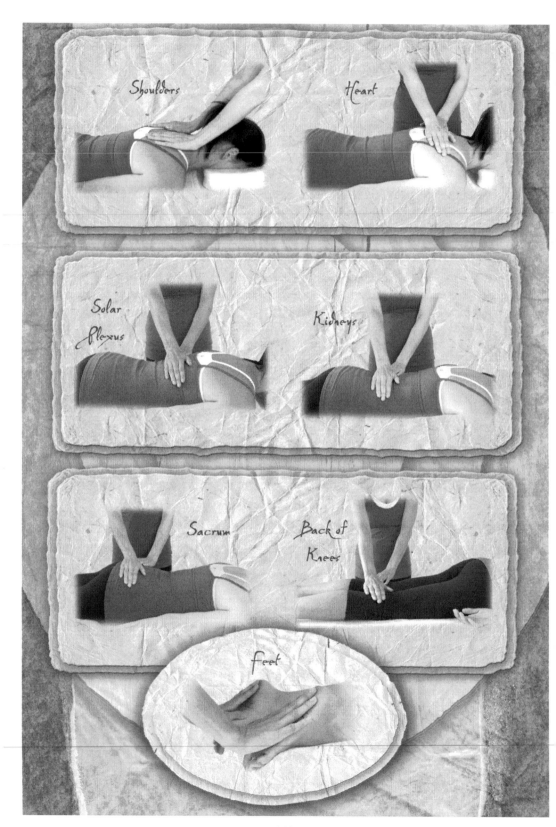

SELF TREATMENT

There is nothing more self-nurturing and loving than to give self-treatment with Reiki. All healing is self-healing and having the ability to connect to Reiki whenever it is required is to me one of the delights of the system. Self-healing can take many forms. A hand placed on the stomach to ease pain, a headache relieved by oneself, a meditation to connect mindfully to what is going on for us that day. Self-healing is part of your self-maintenance program, utilise it daily to ensure your energies are flowing nicely and you are full of vitality.

When approaching self-treatment do so with the same level of care and compassion you would afford someone else. The important thing is to make time for self-treatment and ensure you are able to fully relax without being disturbed. As you develop your self-healing practice, you will discover that each day will bring something different and there will be distinct areas that call for your attention. Approach self-treatment as a mindful practice and if you are lying on the ground, let the earth take what you no longer require to compost for you. The following are a suggested set of hand positions that give you a framework on which to build your self-healing practice. It is not essential to follow them exactly but simply use them as a guide.

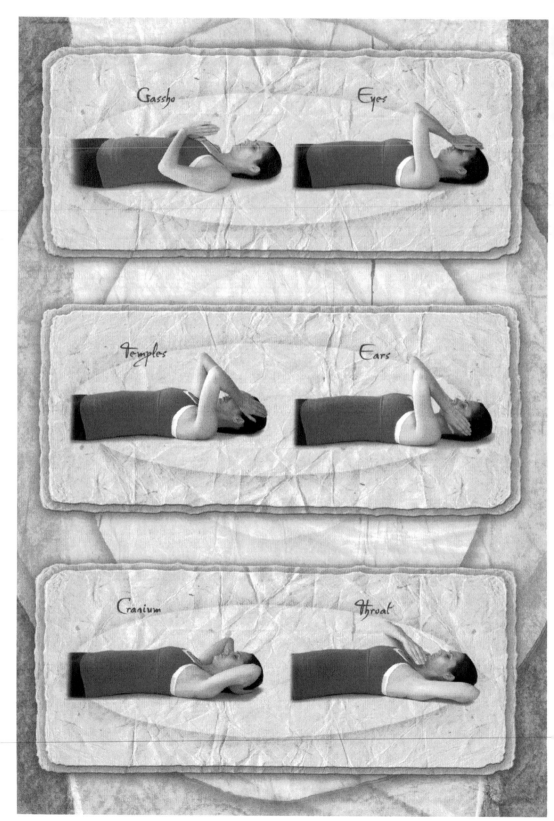

170

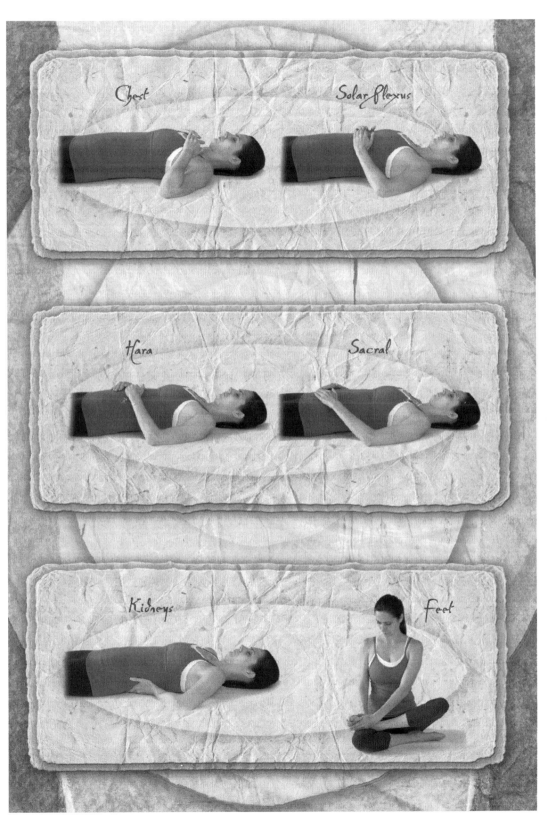

Chest

Solar plexus

Hara

Sacral

Kidneys

Feet

171

SITTING TREATMENT

The call to give Reiki does not always necessitate a formal set up where people come to your clinic and lie on a massage coach. I spent years travelling around the world, making do with what facilities I had. Often the floor was the best place to work from and I was fortunate to be able to crouch for long periods of time. However, not everyone is comfortable lying on the ground and not everyone is comfortable kneeling or crouching for extended periods of time. The sitting treatment is the perfect solution and it offers the additional benefit of being able to work down the front and back of the body at the same time. In terms of clearing the central channel and Chakra system, this is very helpful. This treatment option is particularly useful for a short 30 minutes session. I have found that canvas-backed director's chairs are perfect for the sitting treatment because you can work directly through the canvas. As always, please use the following positions purely as a guide and allow the healing to unfold and be informed by Reiki flow.

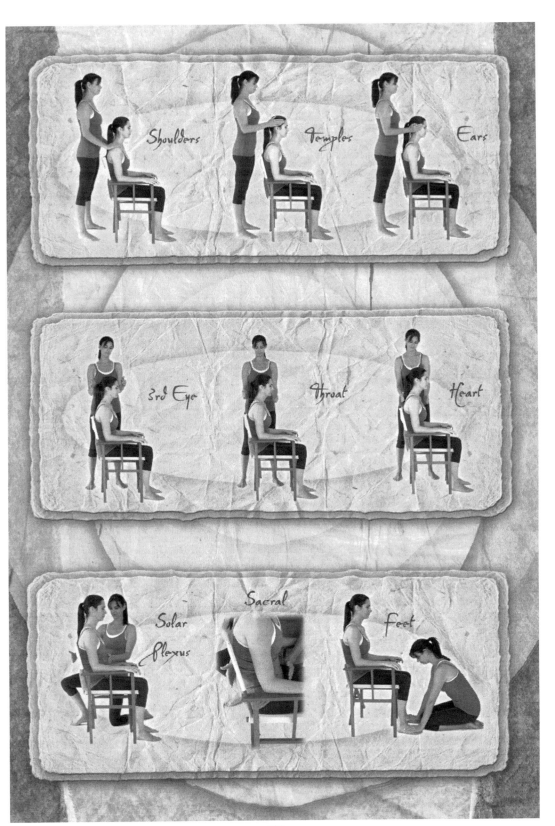

THE MINIMUM CONTENT OF A REIKI 1ST LEVEL TRAINING CLASS

- The History of Reiki

- Definition of Reiki

- Reiki hand circle meditation

- The five principles

- The Reiki 1 Initiations; usually you will receive two if the course is run on a weekend or four if the course is run over four evenings.

- Gassho Meditation

- Preparing before and clearing yourself after giving treatments

- Scanning and intuitive guidance

- A basic understanding of subtle anatomy

- Full treatment positions

- Sitting Treatment positions

- Self treatment positions

- Time given for hands on practice of all course content

- Manual provided

- Certification

REIKI 2ND LEVEL

*"If you always do what you always did
you will always get what you always got"*

The symbols given at this level enable us to explore Reiki in a broader sense. The concept of distant healing is introduced and we are taught the implications of this theory in our everyday life. We are introduced to the idea that our thoughts have a direct bearing on how we feel and what we manifest in our lives. We are shown how to prepare spaces and focus our intent clearly and directly. 2nd Degree Reiki introduces us to the idea that whilst remaining surrendered, we can participate more in our Reiki practice by using our intention.

The 2nd degree offers us the tools to self reflect and modify our lives. We can examine the programmed thoughts, feelings and ideologies that we have inherited and decide if they serve us. It becomes an adventure and a challenge to change un-resourceful behaviour and break down limiting patterns. It is empowering to realise we have the power to change and can take responsibility for the creation of our lives.

The techniques offered in Reiki 2 enable our healing to develop to deeper levels and offers us new approaches of working with our clients. Over the next chapter I will be offering some useful methods that can be incorporated into your healing practice.

CHANGING HABITS

There is no escaping the efficacy of repeated suggestions on a person's psyche, regardless of their emotional state. We live in a world that bombards us with external stimuli suggesting we do this, go here, eat that, think this, wear those, like that, buy this and so on. In effect, expert hypnotists surround us. As a clinical hypnotherapist, I often remark how I have a client for one hour and then I have to send them back to all the other hypnotists in their lives. We are in effect making suggestions all the time both to others and ourselves. Unfortunately, they often take the form of un-resourceful criticisms and judgments. If you have ever listened to your own limiting beliefs, when you are attempting to move out of your comfort zone, you will understand what I mean. In many ways, we are the product of repeated suggestions throughout our lifetime, both internal and external. They have shaped us into who we are and we continue to re-enforce those beliefs creating our futures based on what we believe about ourselves day by day.

One of the delights of Reiki for me is its ability to induce deeply relaxed states in clients. As a hypnotherapist I could be using various techniques to achieve this which centre around guiding the client deeper inside their mind. The premise is that the more deeply relaxed the client, the more readily accepted is the suggestion you give them.

Using Reiki to achieve this feels very natural to me principally because it involves contact with my client and has proved to be highly effective. This method was taught by Hawayo Takata, which she originally referred to as the 'Habit Treatment'. In Japanese it is known as the Seiheki Chiryo Ho where the SHK symbol is used whilst giving suggestions.

This process involves two essential elements. The first, and arguably most important, is to establish an agreed upon affirmation that accurately reflects the client's issue. The second is the installation and repetition of this affirmation.

5 STEPS TO CREATING AFFIRMATIONS

"The thoughts I choose to think and believe right now
are creating my future.
These thoughts form my experiences
tomorrow, next week and next year."

Louise Hay

The most effective way to begin creating an affirmation is to ask your client to tell you about the problem they have. As they begin to talk about it, you will elicit their feelings around the problem. On a big white board and using a marker pen, take notes of what they say about their problem so they can see an evolution of the thought processes taking place.

STEP 1

Ask what the problem is and allow your client time to express it.

Then ask simple questions to expand your understanding of it like;

Q. What kind of?

Q. Is there anything else about it?

Once you have a good foundation of the problem written clearly on the board, your client has an opportunity to look at their thoughts and feelings about the issue.

STEP 2

We then need to establish that the problem and the client are separate things and we do that by asking the following question;

Q. How does it make you feel when you believe that to be true?

This is a clever little question that helps your client to understand that the problem and they are separable and, if they so choose, they can let go of it.

STEP 3

The next step is to find out what it would feel like for them to let go of it.

Ask the following questions and write down the responses;

Q. Can you think of a good reason to hang onto this?

The answer to this question is invariably [NO] because there generally isn't a good reason to hang onto it. But often people persist with particular un-resourceful thought processes to protect themselves in some way. The answer to this question can give you the hidden reason why the client keeps the problem in place. Any affirmation you create has to ensure it replaces the problem with a more resourceful thought or behaviour and satisfies the hidden reason for the problem being there in the first place.

STEP 4

Giving your client an opportunity to imagine life without the problem.

Ask the following question and write down the responses;

Q. Can you imagine what your life would look like if you let go of it?

This question offers your client an opportunity to imagine what life would be like without the problem. It also gives you the foundation on which to build your affirmation.

STEP 5

Allowing the client to feel life without the problem.

Ask the following question and write down the responses;

Q. How will you feel if you let go of it?

This question gives you the feelings that need to be embedded into the affirmation you are creating.

EXAMPLE

STEP 1

What is the problem?

I don't have confidence.

What kind of confidence don't you have?

I am not good enough, not on other's level,
I feel I am not as good as they are.

Is there anything else about confidence?

It's been a problem for years, I am really struggling to change it.

STEP 2

How does it make you feel when you believe that to be true?

Frustrated, upset, angry with myself, paralysed and fearful.

STEP 3

Can you think of a good reason to hang onto this?

No, not really, maybe it keeps me comfortable and safe
[in my comfort zone].

STEP 4

Can you imagine what your life would look like if you let go of it?

I would be able to achieve more and fulfil my potential.

STEP 5

How will you feel if you let go of it?

It would be incredible, exciting, I would feel liberated and powerful.
It would be a lot easier to flow through life.

The answer to the last question in step 1 suggests this is an inner child issue because they have struggled for years with it.

The answer to the question in step 3 is the hidden benefit to her holding the idea she lacks confidence. It communicates the need to feel comfortable and safe. If we can satisfy this need within our affirmation, it will be very effective.

The answer to the question in step 4 gives us her motivations, to fulfil her potential that can be built into the affirmation.

The answer to the question in step 5 gives us the essential feelings required that we can build into the affirmation; feeling incredible, powerful, liberated, excited and in the flow of life.

Finally in crafting an affirmation we want to use our clients' own words so they will more readily accept the affirmation.

THE AFFIRMATION

"It is easy to flow through life
knowing I am safe.
It's incredible how confident and comfortable I am
fulfilling my full potential.
I feel excited, liberated and powerful."

THE HABIT TREATMENT

The treatment can be done in a chair as a stand-alone practice or as part of
a full healing with the client lying down on a treatment table.

Establish with the client what they would like to work on.
Develop an agreed upon positive affirmation or suggestion.
Start with Gassho breathing and see yourself, charged with Reiki.
Stand behind or at the head of your client and place your hands on their
shoulders & visualise CKR.
Place your left hand to the back of the client's head on the occipital ridge.
With your right hand draw or visualise the symbols SHK & CKR over the
3rd eye and place your hand over the forehead. Allow Reiki to flow and
watch for signs of relaxation. Take your time, there is no rush.

Once the client is deeply relaxed read their affirmation out loud
to them as you continue to transmit energy. Repeat this three times
suggesting they take the affirmation deeper inside their mind each time.
They can even repeat it out loud after you.
Finally read their affirmation to them in the second person.

THE AFFIRMATION

"It is easy to flow through life knowing I am safe.
It's incredible how confident and comfortable I am
fulfilling my full potential.
I feel excited, liberated and powerful."

BECOMES

"It is easy to flow through life knowing you are safe.
It's incredible how confident and comfortable you are
fulfilling your full potential.
You feel excited, liberated and powerful."

End by giving thanks with hands in Gassho.

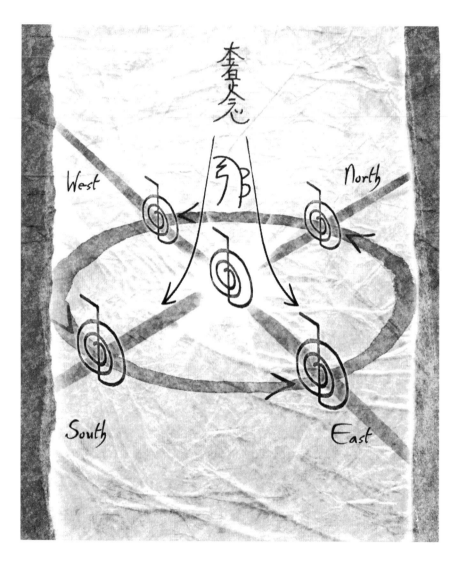

PREPARING A SPACE

PREPARING A SPACE

"Intent reveals desire, action reveals commitment"

Steve Maraboli

The key aspect in manifesting energy for healing is the intention behind it. Just like a shaman's role is to bring spirit to the earth for the purpose of ceremony and ritual, so too is it the Reiki practitioner's role to manifest energy in the here and now for the purpose of healing. Having understood the importance of the elements in terms of a background philosophy to CKR and the manifestation of Reiki, we can begin to integrate this into our preparation practice along with other symbols from Reiki 2nd level. Essentially we are looking to create a space in which healing energy can manifest. This is an energetic space, created through intention and is not determined by the physical space in which it is created. Space preparation clearly falls into the area of intention setting and is intrinsic to the continuity and success of a Reiki practice.

Ideally you will have completed at least Reiki 2nd level training, so that you can use the Reiki symbols as part of your space purification. The three symbols that we use are CKR, SHK and HSZSN.

CKR, Hawayo Takata said meant, "To put the power here" and as such it is useful when preparing a space. When we draw the symbol into our environment we give direction to our intention and can construct energetically a sacred space into which we can manifest the healing and transformative energy of Reiki.

HSZSN, reminds us that there is no separation, and therefore empowers us to use our intention to draw forth our innate connection to the Universal for the purposes of healing.

SHK, can be viewed as symbolic of our intent to purify and cleanse emotional and mental residues that may have become stuck in a space.

Because we are working energetically, it is possible for us to create a personal sacred space for ourself in a large room such as an exhibition hall. For example if you are promoting Reiki in a large area with lots of people around, a harmonised space can be created within that area in which you can operate separate from all the other practitioners and vendors within the room. It is equally possible for you to create a space outdoors, for example the perimeter of a property or an area outdoors where you are performing a ritual. You can define this space first by placing objects on the ground marking the four directions or drawing a circle creating a boundary.

We begin by standing in the centre of the room facing east. Put a CKR into your palms and place your hands in Gassho. When you feel connected, begin the construction of the sacred space by drawing a CKR into a corner of the room, ideally the most easterly, then trace your hands along the walls in an anticlockwise direction to the next corner of the room where you place another CKR. Continue to each corner in turn, repeating all the way around the room until you are back at the original corner where you started and seal your intent with a further placement of CKR.

Then stand in the centre of the room facing the east and tracing from above, draw the HSZSN, SHK and CKR down into the room. It may help to visualise the construction as a pyramid with four sides. Once completed, place your hands in Gassho, invoke Reiki and proceed with Gassho Meditation to build up energy within you and the space. This may be accompanied by visualising light expanding from your heart and filling the space you are working in.

At 3rd level we can introduce the DKM symbol into our space clearing ritual. The essential practice remains the same, we just add the DKM into the four corners of the room or four directions before the CKR symbol.

DISTANT HEALING

"There is no past and there is no present and there is no future,
for even time itself is an illusion and by a single clap of the hand,
it too can be returned to the void".

Mikao Usui

In December 1996 I was in Hawaii having a whale of a time! I was swimming off one of the bubbling black cliffs molded by molten lava being cooled rapidly as it flowed into the sea and forming incredible cascading sculptures. The waves are big in Hawaii and to escape being tossed around on the surface I quickly learnt to dive underwater and come up just for air. Each time I dived down into the depths below me I could hear the orchestral calls of the humpback whales further out to sea. Each year during the winter months the North Pacific humpback whales migrate south to breed, a round trip of approximately 4,000 miles to the Hawaiian Islands. Whales, normally solitary animals, call to each other over 1000's of miles of ocean for the annual gathering.

The Whale is regarded as a powerful totem animal in many indigenous cultures and when we hear its call, it is said to reconnect us to the depths of our being, to remind us of our origins and open ourselves to the universal unfolding. Whale people are said to be telepathic and can tune into the emotional frequencies that reveal our interconnectedness to everything. As I dived down into the depths, I was deeply touched by their calls, I felt myself connected not only to them but also to the ocean, the islands and the elements all around me.

It hadn't started out like that! Hours after arriving in Hawaii from a teaching tour in Boston, my upper back had gone into spasm right behind my heart centre. My first four days had involved a painful routine of going to the chiropractor in the morning and lying flat on my back in agony in the afternoon. "Great" I thought, "two weeks in Hawaii and I can't move!" I was surrounded by healers and despite their best efforts I was seriously stuck! Finally on the fifth day I had arrived at the chiropractors to find he wasn't there and had left a colleague to see me. She was softly spoken and asked me to lie on a therapy couch and asked me what was going on. As I explained what had happened she placed her hand gently on the centre of my chest as if to get a sense of the cause of my pain. She then simply said, "It's as if a spear is stuck through you!" Instantly a huge spasm went through me lifting my legs off the table and when they came back down with a thud, my body shook violently for several minutes. Afterwards as I lay there she said "Wow, that was different!"

I started laughing from relief, because I knew the stuck-ness in my back had gone and the pain that had been locked in had been replaced by vibrations as the released energy was suddenly free to flow. That night I had a powerful dream of being killed in another time by a spear being stabbed through my heart. There was another man killed in the dream with me and I felt I was responsible for his death. I recognised him as my father in this life.

Before I had left for Hawaii I had given my father his first ever Reiki treatment for long-standing pain in his right shoulder. During the treatment I had seen my paternal grandfather and when the treatment had ended, I asked him if he had been thinking of his father. He seemed quite shocked and said he had seen a vision of him holding both our arms as if to pull us together. As I digested the dream and remembered the treatment I had given my father I realised the pain in the back of my heart was the grief I had felt as a young boy being sent from my home in Africa to a boarding school in England. It had galvanised a great deal of separation between my father and me and I understood in that moment I had to heal my inner child.

It is said whale medicine can help us understand on a deeper level the causes of unrest in our daily lives. It is not easy to track the emotional origin of inner turmoil, forgive and move on from experiences that have left a stain on our lives. But Nelson Mandela once said of his ability to forgive his captors "holding onto resentment is like drinking poison and expecting the other person to die." Forgiveness is our ability to retrieve the lost and fragmented aspects of our lives and make ourselves whole once again.

I resolved right then to heal myself and knew that Reiki was the vehicle to do it. The method I used occurred to me one day whilst looking through a family photo album. I came across a double page where on the left side there was a picture of me before I had left Africa for boarding school and on the right side a photograph taken on the day I went to school in my new uniform. I couldn't believe the difference in the demeanour of the two children I was looking at, one outgoing and powerful, the other frightened and withdrawn. I developed an inner child method, which I published in my first book, Practical Reiki, using distant healing methods and photographs of people they selected of themselves from their childhood. The process was fairly simple, using the photograph and distant healing to open a portal for dialogue with the inner child and provide the space for emotional expression and needs in order for healing to occur. I will share it again at the end of this chapter in more detail and urge you to use it for yourself and your clients and students.

Considering the short time I spent in Hawaii, the experiences I had there shaped my relationship to energy in many ways. A few days before leaving I had an experience that revealed how we influence our realities depending upon the clarity of our intentions. I was invited with a friend to go on a free dive trip in Molokini crater off the coast of Maui. The crater is a Marine Preserve and features one of the most pristine hard coral reefs in Hawaii. It is teeming with tropical fish, rays, octopi, moray eels and white tip reef sharks. It is effectively a submerged volcanic cinder cone and because of its protection from the outside tides, visibility can exceed 100 feet or more. We were finding it hard to contain our excitement. Unfortunately both of us were scheduled to fly back to the west coast the day before the trip. We were on separate airlines and both made calls to see if we could postpone our flights to later in the week. Things seemed to be against us as we were informed a snowstorm had hit the west coast causing flight disruptions and we were told it would be impossible to change our seats. Somewhat disgruntled we looked at each other thinking that was it, no dive trip! I don't know if it was the Hawaiian effect on us but a few minutes later we both said the same thing. "Lets send Reiki to the situation!" We set about creating a healing ritual to clear all resistance to us being able to change our flights and proceeded to send energy for ten minutes. Afterwards we both called our airlines and guess what? Yep we both managed to change our bookings.

The translation of the mantra Hon Sha Ze Sho Nen that resonates with me most is; "The origin of all, the essence of our being is pure consciousness." The process of Distant Healing learnt in 2nd level Reiki at a deeper level, helps us to realise our interconnectedness with everything around us.

Using distant healing practices helps us to understand the impact our intentions and thoughts have on our own lives and the world we choose to experience. They offer us a method through which we can refocus our intent and modify our thoughts and feelings towards specific events regardless of where they may exist. Ultimately it is in the present moment that we experience things and by changing our relationship towards past experiences and future events we allow ourselves to rest more completely in the NOW. Distant Healing also offers us an opportunity to recognise our connection to people not physically present and to send positive thoughts and energy to them.

Distant Mudra

On page 202 I will be discussing how in some lineages of Reiki, mudras have been integrated into the practice like the one above used for distant healing.

THE DISTANT HEALING RITUAL

When sending distant healing it is important to create a space that enables you to open up to Reiki without fear of being disturbed. The recipient does not have to be aware of the time you will connect to them, but it can be helpful for them to utilise the energy to the best effect if they are. Some teachers suggest asking for permission, however the exceptions would be emergencies and if the person is unavailable or deceased. Go through the procedure of invocation and preparing your space as if you were doing a session one to one. Set the intention by drawing the symbols HSZSN & CKR into your hands and do Gassho Meditation to focus and generate energy. If visualising the person, give Reiki to your eyes first. If you have a photograph of the person place it so that you can focus on them. The distant healing symbol 3 and power symbol 1 will suffice but I generally include the mental/emotional symbol 2. The sequence is as follows;

STATE THE NAME OF PERSON 3 TIMES

CKR 3 TIMES

HSZSN 3 TIMES

SHK 3 TIMES

CKR 3 TIMES

One method is to draw with your right hand whilst leaving your left hand palm up on your lap. Once drawn or visualized, leave your right hand palm forward shoulder height as if to direct energy whilst visualising the person or simply focusing on the photograph or object you have in front of you. Hold your attention on the person for approximately 10 minutes. You can also intend the Reiki extends into the person's environment and the session may finish there. Draw a CKR in reverse spiralling out from the centre to disconnect and then bring your hands into Gassho to give thanks and blessings.

You may send distant healing in the same way to an event that may be in your past or future. Simply follow the same procedure as above using, your intention to focus on the event that you wish to send energy to.

BEAMING ENERGY

The first time I experienced the power of beaming I was the recipient not the person giving the energy. I was lying on my back under a garden pagoda receiving a group healing from four people. To my surprise the person I was most aware of wasn't physically near me. Throughout the session I was acutely aware of this person and once the session had finished, I sat up to look around to see where they were. To my surprise they were sitting on a rock about 50 meters away with their eyes closed.

Beaming energy is a useful method when you either wish to tune into a session from a distance or send Reiki to someone or something that you cannot directly touch. Examples could be an accident scene, a distressed horse, a wild animal, or a room full of people. I have used it in many ways, from calming a distressed German shepherd on the London Underground to connecting to someone in one of my classes that I feel is close to an emotional release and may need supporting.

To beam energy, remembering your intention and focus is the key. Decide where you wish to send the energy and visualise the HSZSN, SHK & CKR symbols. You can either close your eyes and visualise where you are sending the energy, or keep your eyes open and look at where you wish to send energy. If you are near enough and in a private healing space, you can direct energy through the palms of your hands towards the person.

HEALING CONFLICTS OR OBSTACLES

Using the distant healing symbols we can target particular problems that have come to represent obstacles in our lives. We can use Reiki to bring about shifts in our perspective and the way our conditioned responses to a situation cause us to act. These issues may take the form of conflicts in relationships or in the work place or simply be things that appear as repeating patterns in our lives. The more we embrace Reiki as a life path, the more desire we have to dissolve conflicts and ensure we live in harmony with those around us. As we are the only thing we can control in terms of our own behaviour or response to situations, it is a good idea to start with ourselves. The easiest way to do this is to gain some distance and perspective from the issue. When we are embroiled in the drama of conflict we are just in it and far too close to have a healthy viewpoint.

The first step then is to disassociate ourselves by seeing the issue or conflict out there. It is effective to put that part of ourselves on a screen so we can watch ourselves as if in a movie theatre. Once we are able to do that and observe the drama as if it is happening to someone else, we can utilise the distant healing ritual and send healing to the situation. With practice this visualisation can become a very effective tool for personal transformation.

USING THE TELEPHONE OR VIDEO CALL

Interestingly when Hawayo Takata taught distant healing practices she often referred to them as the 'telephone dial'. It has become increasingly popular in these busy times to use telephones or Skype for one to one sessions particularly in life coaching. These therapeutic tools can also be utilised for Reiki sessions. Both are fantastic communication tools and I am sure you have all experienced consoling someone on the phone and simultaneously feeling their emotions whilst talking to them. It is just as easy to empathise over the phone or through Skype than if someone is physically present. The important thing to remember is it is a two-way conversation and it is just as possible to send positive calming healing energy to someone as it is to feel emotionally charged states. I use these modern devices to connect and will then utilise intention and distant healing practices to send healing wherever it is needed. Often people report feeling heat descend on them and warmth in the heart as they are on the phone. It is a very simple and effective way to work.

MANIFESTATION

As I discussed in the symbology section of this book, I believe the distant healing symbol was given by Mikao Usui to teach us the interconnectedness of everything. Through our practice we learn how to align ourselves to flow and, as a consequence, realise what we manifest in our lives is a reflection of that flow. Manifestation occurs regardless of what we are thinking and feeling, but manifesting happiness requires us to think happy thoughts and feel happy feelings. To live in accordance with the five principles is a simple way to invite blessings into our lives.

JUST FOR TODAY

DO NOT ANGER

DO NOT WORRY

BE GRATEFUL

WORK DILIGENTLY

BE KIND TO ALL LIVING THINGS

To invite blessings [to manifest and attract what we desire] we are essentially saying we must dissolve anger, bring ourselves into the present, be grateful for what we have, work honestly and be kind. When we do that, we naturally align ourselves to the good in our lives and as a consequence we manifest more of it. There are many manifestation rituals that we could do with distant healing in mind but I would suggest by first ensuring we are present and grateful for the miracles of our lives, we will quite naturally attract more happiness into them. What you give energy to becomes your reality, so ensure you notice what is good in your life and you may find you begin attracting more of it.

A SIMPLE MANIFESTATION RITUAL

Take a large piece of paper and draw a large circle on it.

Fold the paper in half and in half again.

Then unfold it and where there are creases draw four CKR's
within the circle.

In the middle of the circle put what you wish to attract more of.

Let your creative side enjoy this and use colors, symbols, affirmations
and drawings. Make sure you stay within the circle.

When you are happy with it write or draw outside of the circle
all the things that stop you achieving this.
Be honest with yourself use black pens
to contrast the bright colors inside the circle.

When you are happy you have included everything sit back and look at it.

Notice how much attention you give to the things outside of the circle
compared to the things inside the circle. Sadly usually people give the
most energy to things outside the circle. Is it any wonder then that
nothing in the circle is being manifest?

Take a pair of scissors and cut around the colorful circle
separating it from the resistance around it.

On the back of the circle draw the Reiki symbols,

HSZSN, SHK & CKR.

Place the circle on a wall in your home so you can see it daily.

You can then place the paper with the resistance
written in black ink in a fire.

Watch as it burns and imagine all the resistance
being consumed by the fire.

After three months, notice if more of what you wished to attract
is now in your life.

RETRIEVING LOST AND FRAGMENTED PARTS OF OURSELVES

There are many techniques designed around the notion, that revisiting emotional events in a therapeutic environment, enables a person to bring them to the surface and let them go. It is widely considered that emotion held by the body gives rise to postural distortion as it naturally contracts around an emotional impact. E-motion is often considered to be energy in its natural state of motion and it is considered unhealthy for emotional energy to become stuck or repressed.

Over many years of therapy I have seen that a healing is often accompanied by spontaneous abreaction and the sudden recall of suppressed memories can accompany such releases. I have had to weigh up the benefits therapeutically of re-experiencing the accompanying negative emotion, against the potential damage caused by keeping it in.

There are concerns when guiding people into past trauma, in particular, false memories being planted into the minds of vulnerable clients which can have serious consequences. Deliberately focusing a patient's attention on an emotional impact can bring to the surface negative emotions which may have already been dealt with and leave a person feeling violated and misunderstood.

The danger comes when a therapist leads a person to where they believe a problem exists, rather than gradually exposing them to the core memory in a gradual way. It is therefore important to ensure they feel able to manage the experience at all times and to guide them gently to find the emotional memory that requires releasing. The adoption of a client-centered approach to therapy must be viewed as prudent, to avoid leading a patient deliberately to a desired memory for the sole purpose of creating abreaction. Or more worryingly planting the seeds of false memory that could have long-term consequences.

Before we start, it helps to set up a safe place anchor we can utilise in the event our client feels overwhelmed emotionally. Asking the client to describe a happy peaceful memory first can also establish a similar safe place, which they can retreat back to if necessary.

Combining Reiki with photographs of ourselves as children is an effective way to reclaim fragmented aspects of our lives and reform connections to the spirit of our childhood. As Reiki is present we can ensure a safe and supportive environment to whatever may arise whilst exploring issues.

The unconscious mind has the ability to offer up the right memory at the right time. As therapists we have to learn to trust in the bodies natural ability to heal itself and ensure we only guide a client to discover what they need to release and not forcefully lead them somewhere they don't need to go.

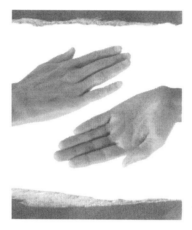

Remember this is an opportunity to heal past patterns so that loving connections can be re established both within ourselves and with those around us.

Please note this is a way to utilise distant healing that has proved effective for me personally and a method I devised myself. It does not relate to Hawayo Takatas original teachings as far as I know.

The exercise can be done one to one or in a group.

If working as a group establish a connection and intention by holding hands in a Reiki circle with recipient in the centre. Ask the person who they would like to join them in the circle and act as their support anchor.

If working alone, place your hands in Gassho to set your intention before beginning and act as both the guide and support.

INNER CHILD EXERCISE

Establish a safety anchor by touching the front and back of the heart of recipient and state their name out loud three times followed by the absent healing sequence - CKR, HSZSN, SHK, CKR

Release safety anchor and proceed as follows.

Ask the recipient to look at the picture they have brought and ask the following questions

Q. Describe the child in the picture

Q. What memories/feelings come up as you look at him/her?

Q. What do you see, feel and hear?

Q. Who else comes up in the memories/feelings?

Q. What does he/she need?

Q. Can the adult you give that to him/her now? If yes go ahead

Often what is needed is integration of the adult and inner child and I have found the most effective way to do that is to ask the person this question.

Q. Can you embrace him/her and bring them into your heart?

Do not push people to do this until they feel absolutely ready to do so. If they say they are unable, ask them what needs to happen first. When they are ready to embrace and have done so, proceed as follows.

Q. Imagine the two of you integrated and reconnected

Q. Are you now ready to leave that in the past and move on?

Q. Only when you are truly ready, imagine coming back together to the present moment more aware.

Q. Nod your head when you have done that

Touch the safety anchor to ground them into the NOW.

Hands in Gassho to give thanks.

THE MINIMUM CONTENT OF A REIKI 2ND LEVEL TRAINING CLASS

- Review of prior Reiki learning and experiences since last course.

- The 2nd level Reiki symbols, origins, meanings and uses.

- The Habit Treatment with symbols

- Space clearing and creating a healing space

- Opening and closing a Reiki treatment with CKR

- One Reiki Initiation where the symbols are placed into the hands.

- Distant healing practices

- Further Reiki techniques

- Information on duty of care and professional responsibilities

- Time given for hands on practice of all course content

- Manual provided

- Certification

REIKI 3RD LEVEL

Traditionally Hawayo Takata taught Reiki in just three levels, with the 3rd level being an inclusive training with a view to becoming a teacher of Reiki. An extended period of practice was required between 2nd level and 3rd levels and usually the students participation in 3rd level was at their teacher's discretion.

Most modern teachers of Reiki now teach it in four levels with the 3rd level regarded as the advanced practitioner and 4th level the master teacher. The contents of 3rd level courses therefore vary depending on how the teacher chooses to distribute them across the 3rd and 4th levels.

As a guide the 3rd level is seen as a consolidation and review of techniques and practices already learnt with the addition of the master symbol and initiation. There may also be some extra techniques learnt such as; object clearing and blessing, using the breath and more particular techniques that can be applied in treatments.

With so much new research being done into Reiki many teachers find there is always more information that can be passed onto their students.

With an open mind in the following chapter, I run through some of the traditional techniques but also some of the non traditional. In particular I discuss mudras and how I have found them to be of benefit when integrated into a Reiki practice.

DANTIAN BRIDGE

When I learnt Reiki, my master, June Woods, taught me a practice, which involved placing one hand underneath the client whilst they laid on their back and the other just below the belly button. I was interested to find out that some of the modern Japanese systems are doing a similar practice called Gedoku Chiryo Ho. 'Doku' means toxin and 'Ge' means to bring down. It is described as a detoxification process whereby the toxins are imagined to leave the body and flow into the earth. As we have learnt, the Lower Dantian or Seika Tanden in the Hara is an important reservoir for vital energy to be gathered. It is also an important place for us to focus our intention particularly through the breath. Mindful awareness of this area creates stillness and, by virtue, clarity. Similar to a jam jar filled with muddy water, which clears when left still.

If we look into the subtle anatomy of this practice we find it has more benefits than simply detoxification. The exact position of the hand at the back corresponds to the 'Ming Men' GV4 acupoint associated with the "Sea of Yang" heavenly energy representing one's relation to spirit. It is known as the 'Gate of Vitality' or 'Life Gate' and is an important point for body warmth and vitality. Giving Reiki to this area primes the body's major energetic pump so that Qi can spread more efficiently throughout the body. This benefits the whole system, in particular the immune system.

The front hand is laid just below the belly button, which corresponds to three acupoints. 'Guanyuan' 'Shimen' and 'Qi Hai' CV4, CV5 and CV6. These acupoints are associated with the "Sea of Yin" earthly energy, representing ones relation to the earth. These are important points for fortifying the Jing Essence and Original Qi. They are also the main points to strengthen and support kidney function, aid digestion and address weaknesses or dormancy in the whole body. When treating this area it is important to remember that these acupoints are only gates to an energetic field and the real Dantian and Ming Men lie somewhere deeper within the body.

As the Dantian Bridge focuses energy into the 'Ming Men' which helps to circulate Qi around the microcosmic orbit, it can be helpful to suggest to your client to breathe deeply and consciously into the 'Hara', which serves to bring fresh vital energy into the system. As a word of caution, this can be a very powerful technique, resulting in strong abreactions for some people. In the event of this happening, the client may experience strong tingling sensations throughout the body, which are usually more concentrated in the hands and jaw. If this should occur, it will possibly leave the person feeling emotional but after a short while it will subside and in time they will feel highly rejuvenated.

Hawayo Takata always suggested treating the whole body whenever possible and so I suggest incorporating the Dantian Bridge into a full healing treatment.

The client needs to be lying on their back and be nicely relaxed. Sitting on their right side, slide your left hand under their lower back between the second and third lumbar vertebrae. Advise your client to allow their full weight to rest on your hand. Place your right hand just below the belly button and allow Reiki to flow. If you have practitioner level Reiki 2 utilise SHK and CKR. Take the energy down the legs to the feet to complete.

Dantian Bridge

MUDRAS

At first glance and somewhat surprisingly, Mudras have not appeared to be included in the original Usui Reiki Ryoho. One would have thought with a hands on healing technique such as Reiki that incorporated symbolism and mantras into its system, Mudras would have been utilised too. A Mudra [mu-dra] 'seal', 'mark' or 'gesture' is a symbolic gesture normally formed by the hands and fingers and found in Hinduism and Buddhism. They are regarded as spiritual gestures of divine origin.

It is possible they occurred to reflect the quality of inner states achieved during meditations. I like this idea because I myself have witnessed, during treatments, moments where the hands spontaneously express different qualities of energy as if forming Mudras; the hands and fingers involuntarily being moved and molded into shapes by the energy flowing through them.

THE GASSHO

When we look a little closer at our Reiki training, we may recognise that we have regularly incorporated at least one Mudra into our practice, from our very first initiation.

During the initiation we are asked to form this Mudra over our heart and over our mind and later it becomes integrated into our meditations and treatments. Gassho is a traditional gesture formed by placing the palms of the hands together with all fingers pointing upwards. It symbolises the oneness of all beings and is often used in the East as a humble greeting, a sign of respect or to give thanks. Called Namaste in Sanskrit. ['Namah' means bow 'te' means to you]. It literally means, "I bow to you" and is regarded as an honouring of the divinity in someone we meet. The two hands brought together are symbolic of our earthly human nature meeting our heavenly Buddha nature. The left hand represents our human nature and the right hand our Buddha nature. Brought together over the heart or mind it is symbolic that both aspects reside within us and on the path to enlightenment, we are never far away from our Buddha self. It is also symbolic of the polarities of Yin and Yang, heaven and earth brought into balance through our loving intention to create Qi.

It is so incredibly valuable to our practice and as well as serving to generate energy flow this Mudra can be used in many other ways. The Gassho Mudra is a place where we invoke spirit and honour the elements of consciousness and light, bringing them into the five elements of our physical self. It is a place where we can honour our ancestral lineage and where our intention is established. For example, tracing a CKR into our Lao Gong and bringing our hands together immediately reflects the intention of CKR which is to bring the seven elements of the universe into harmony and balance right here right now! We can set the intention for any treatment we are about to begin by tracing the relevant symbol combination into the palms and placing our hands into Gassho. If we are giving the Habit Treatment, we can draw the SHK and CKR symbols into our palms to establish connection and intent. If it is distant healing we wish to do, then we can place HSZSN and CKR into our palms. Whether we are giving the initiations, blessing an object or giving any of the treatments, we can first set the intention in Gassho.

In Vedic tradition, each finger of the hand represents an element and is connected to an energy centre. It is believed by placing different fingers together through Mudras, the elements are balanced and the electromagnetic system is revitalised.

THE FINGERS - ELEMENTS - CHAKRAS.

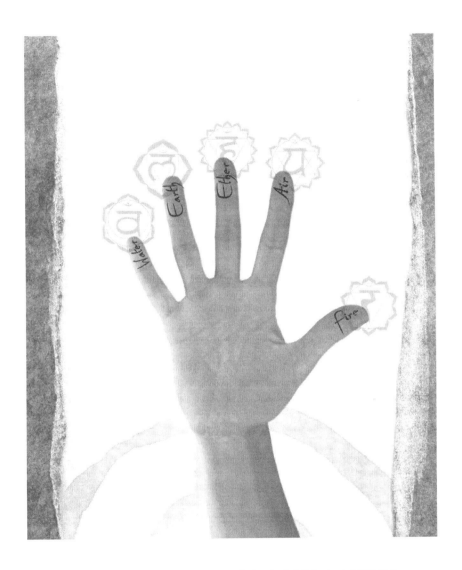

THE THUMB - ELEMENT FIRE - CHAKRA MANIPURA

INDEX FINGER - ELEMENT AIR - CHAKRA ANAHATA

MIDDLE FINGER - ELEMENT ETHER - CHAKRA VISHUDDHI

RING FINGER - ELEMENT EARTH - CHAKRA MULADHARA

LITTLE FINGER - ELEMENT WATER, CHAKRA SVADHISTHANA

THE HEAVEN AND EARTH MUDRA

There is one other Mudra I wish to discuss here which is used by Reiki masters during the initiations. It has its roots in Qigong and is one of the brocades in the Baduanjin sequence, which is one of the oldest forms of 5 Elements Qigong. Not all initiation ceremonies I have come across include this Mudra and certainly, in the simplified Reiju empowerments from Japan that I have seen, it is not included. Quite how or why it became part of the initiation process is unclear to me but in terms of being symbolic of the intention required in passing attunements, it is very clear and very powerful.

The Mudra when used in Reiki attunements requires the left hand to be raised to the heavens with the palm facing skywards thumb forwards and the fingers pointing in towards an imaginary mid line running upwards from the crown. The right hand palm is facing the earth at hip height, normally with fingers pointing forwards away from the body.

In the Reiki initiation, the raised left hand is symbolic of receiving the connection from spirit and the lower right hand is placed over the crown as a conduit, delivering the Reiki phenomenon through the central channel of the initiate to be grounded through their energetic system.

MUDRAS ADDED TO THE REIKI SYSTEM

There are other Mudras that have been incorporated into the Reiki practice through various branches, some I recognise from Qigong practices. It is difficult to discuss them without stepping away from the authenticity of the Reiki system but I do wish to examine them in more detail out of curiosity. I will discuss various ways that they can be incorporated into the Reiki practice but it is important to remember they are not traditional elements taught by Hawayo Takata.

There are two Mudras I wish to discuss here directly associated with the cosmic Buddha Dainichi Nyorai, one of which 'The Chiken in Mudra' or 'Mudra of the Wisdom Fist' I have already examined in the symbology section. Despite providing some interesting connections from a philosophical perspective there is little benefit that I have found in holding this Mudra when giving Reiki. Instead the other Mudra associated with Dainichi Nyorai I have experienced to be of benefit in particular when combined with Gassho. It is known as the Sun Mudra.

I first came across the Sun Mudra in Qigong with a teacher in Italy in the mid 1990's. It was part of a sequence that we used to bring the light of the sun into our crown or hearts. The Mudras connection to the cosmic Buddha and possible relationship to the shining bright light of DKM motivated me to experiment with it. Intuitively I began combining it with Gassho to plant symbols with the breath.

Sun Mudra

THE OM MUDRA

"Om is the bow, the individual self is the arrow, the spirit is the target. It should be pierced with an unfaltering aim. One should then become one with it like the arrow that has penetrated the target"

Verse from the Mundaka Upanishad

The Om Mudra, like the Sun Mudra, is not part of the original Usui Reiki Ryoho. Its addition here is owed in part to its association with the Taoist philosophy of the empty void 'Wu', from which the oneness 'Taiji' is birthed. Also to the link the Om Mudra has to Amida Nyorai and by association the SHK symbol. The Om Mudra like SHK has a calming effect on the mind and is said to help concentrate the attention on the idea of the divine.

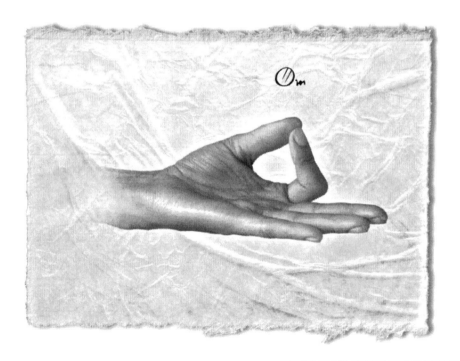

The Om Mudra symbolises the union of the individual and cosmic self. The Mudras purpose is to aid the development of self-awareness and identify oneself with the pure non-verbal feeling of delight that arises out of realising oneself as being interwoven with Divine Spirit. It is achieved by placing the tip of the index finger against the tip of the thumb of the same hand forming a circle symbolizing union, unity or oneness. The remaining three fingers are held together pointing straight.

Amida Nyorai is often seen depicted with both hands in OM brought together to form a Mudra known as the 'Mida-no-join Mudra'. The middle, ring and little fingers of both hands lie on top of one another, with the thumbs and index finger of both hands touching each other, forming circles. The left hand represents human nature and is placed palm upwards underneath the right hand symbolising the Buddha nature. Both index fingers and tips of the thumbs touching form two circles. The joining of the two Om Mudras expresses unity and reveals symbolically that Buddha consciousness resides within each of us.

The Om Mudra represents the transcendence and liberation of the ego self resting in the heart, the meeting place of heaven and earth. In alchemy, fire is the element into which base metals are placed in order to turn them to gold and air is the element that fans the flames of fire. The Mudra brings together the elements of fire and air, which relate to the Solar Plexus Chakra [Manipura] and the Heart Chakra [Anahata]. Manipura means 'the place of jewels' and is the body's alchemical fire that burns away all impurities leaving just the purity of the golden self. This dissolution of the lower aspects of ego being transformed and purified allows for a more complete union with the spiritual self, like the phoenix in the flames the ego is reborn, stripped of its self-importance and fully surrendered as a servant of spirit into the heart. Anahata means 'that which is ever new' and as our breath brings us into the now moment the heart is metaphorically where we let go into flow and merge with our divine nature.

OM MEDITATION

Whilst seated or in the lotus position, place your hands in the 'Amida Jo in' Mudra and bring your awareness to your breath.

Relax your breathing into the Seika Danten and drop into your body fully

Then bring your attention to your Heart Chakra in the centre of your chest [not your physical heart]

Be aware of yourself breathing through the heart then imagine a smiling radiant form in your chest that represents your divine nature

See and feel the radiance as loving, calm and peaceful

Continue to meditate upon it

CHAKRA BALANCE WITH OM MUDRA

With regard the use of the Om Mudra therapeutically;
I suggest doing a Chakra balancing exercise on your clients
whilst forming this Mudra with your hands.

Stand on the right of your client

Form the Om with each hand and place over the body,
the right hand over the 1st Chakra and the left hand over the 6th Chakra.
You may also visualise SHK and CKR.

Then move your hands together, the right hand to the 2nd Chakra and the
left hand to the 5th Chakra, visualise again the SHK and CKR.

Finally bring your right hand over the 3rd Chakra and left hand over the
4th Chakra. Visualise SHK and CKR again.

Hold in each position for approximately 1 - 2 minutes
or until you feel to move on.

THE ABSENT HEALING MUDRA

Distant Mudra

Earlier when discussing distant healing, I recommended placing your left hand palm up on your lap and tracing the distant healing symbols with your right hand held at chest height. This is a Mudra that is related to giving and receiving. It is a smaller more contained adaptation to the Heaven and Earth Mudra used by some western lineages for attunement. The left hand facing up receives the flow of energy from spirit and the right hand palm facing forward directs that flow of energy to where the intention is set. The right hand is used to trace the distant healing symbols and is then held to the right of the chest at the level of the Heart Chakra and directs the healing.

CLEARING THE CENTRAL CHANNEL

A clear central channel enables better energy flow between heaven and earth and plays an essential part in supporting a person's journey towards fulfillment of their own potentiality. Cleansing allows the energy system to be harmonised and according to Chakra theory provides the best environment for self-development to occur. Chakra theory suggests refinement of the self through meditation and spiritual discipline allows the awakening of the electric, fiery spiritual force known as Kundalini, which lies asleep, like a coiled serpent in the base of the spine. When aroused it uncoils and ascends the central channel as the male and female serpents Ida and Pingala, the energy content of the vital body rising as the individuals awareness evolves.

It may be useful at this point to remember the relationship we have considered between the Reiki symbols. Working together they symbolise the purification of the mental and emotional obstructions held within the energetic system creating harmony and flow. This allows consciousness to be raised into higher states of awareness. On a practical level, when we clear mental and emotional obstructions in the system, energy is free to flow through the central channel promoting vitality, health and wellbeing.

Archetypically this is symbolised by the peacock transmuting the snakes poisons and the snake rising up from its earthly realm to gain a new higher perspective of reality. We find the same symbolism in the transformation of ignorance and negativity by Amida Nyora and other Bosatsu into enlightened states of mind. Again in the heavenly garden of E-din [abode of the rightful ones], the serpent [creative life force] is coiled around the tree of life and knowledge [the central channel] symbolizing the rise of consciousness.

If we look at the development of the Reiki hand positions over time, we can see they follow a pattern determined by the location of the Chakras. Regardless of our beliefs about Chakras, we can hopefully see the value in enabling energy to flow more freely through our clients central channels. The full treatment naturally achieves this because we are working on the primary areas that require release. We can also employ our intention whilst seated at the head of our client and visualise the symbols passing into the crown or utilize the sun mudra as follows.

PLANTING SYMBOLS

Mikao Usui was reported to have said that you can give Reiki with your breath if you feel heat in your chest. There is a similar method in some Japanese systems called 'Koki Ho' which follows a similar ethos with the practitioner breathing from the lower abdomen and exhaling gently to the area in need of treatment. Hawayo Takata apparently taught level 2 students how to heal with the breath and certainly master students to pass initiation using the breath.

Draw into your palms with your dominant hand the symbol sequence that reflects the intention you have. Place your hands into Gassho in front of your heart, relax your breathing into your Seika Tanden and concentrate on your heart and hands during the outbreath.

Once you feel an abundance of energy in your heart and palms, part your hands and blow through the palms into the crown and then form the Sun Mudra and allow the radiance of Reiki to flow through the central channel. It helps to visualise this pathway becoming clear all the way down to the base of the spine.

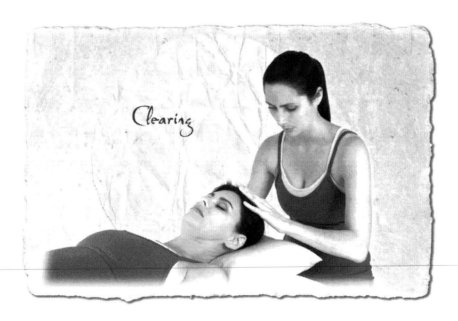

Clearing

BLESSING OBJECTS

Most people are today familiar with the researcher Masaru Emoto who sadly passed away on the 17th October 2014. His research featured in the movie 'What The Bleep Do We know'. His experiments into the affects of intention upon water have inspired millions to appreciate water in a new light and helped them to realise the power thoughts and intent have upon our environment and our health.

Lawrence Ellyard, a Reiki Master and student of Masaru Emoto, plus other members of the International Institute for Reiki Training, had the opportunity to participate in a scientific experiment on how Reiki affects Tokyo tap water. Up to that point Tokyo tap water had never formed hexagonal ice crystals that Masaru Emoto had become famous for. It was believed the heavy chlorine content and distorted vibration of Tokyo's water source, prevented the formation of the crystals. To obtain an ice crystal from Tokyo tap water using only Reiki energy would be a world first. The experiment was conducted by seven Reiki practitioners, who formed a circle and directed energy [through the sun mudra interestingly], without physically touching the water sample. The results revealed several ice crystal formations and one in particular showed a seven-sided formation, which was interesting due to seven Reiki practitioners participating in the water blessing.

The inclusion of the DKM symbol into our practice enables us to bestow blessings. Typically these take the form of initiations. However blessings can be given to anything from a boat being launched to a meal being served. In terms of incorporating blessings into our healing practice, DKM can be used to bless crystals before placing them on to the body, water before drinking, room sprays made with essential oils, the person lying on the therapy couch themselves, the room the person is lying in or any other object or thing that you can think of.

To bless an object, if small enough, place it into the palm of your left hand and draw the DKM, SHK and CKR symbols over the object with your right hand, then place your hands together and bring into Gassho over your heart. Breathe to your Seika Tanden on the in breath and to your heart on the outbreath. Feel the abundance of energy in your heart and palms infusing the object. Seal with a CKR to finish.

For larger objects or for a group blessing create the intention by placing the DKM, SHK and CKR symbols into your palms and place into Gassho. Breathe to your Seika Tanden on the in breath and to your heart on the outbreath. When you feel an abundance of energy in your heart and palms, part your hands and blow through the palms and then form the Sun Mudra and allow the radiance of Reiki to flow. Seal with CKR to finish.

Blessing Objects

REIKI LOVE SPRAY

MAKE YOUR OWN REIKI LOVE SPRAY.
IN AN OLD SPRAY BOTTLE MIX WATER
WITH A FEW DROPS OF ESSENTIAL OIL OF YOUR CHOICE,
ROSE AND LAVENDER IS A NICE COMBINATION.
STICK ON A LABEL WITH DKM, SHK AND CKR
DRAWN UPON IT. SPRAY ANYTIME
YOU NEED A REIKI SPACE.

THE MINIMUM CONTENT OF A REIKI 3ᴿᴰ LEVEL TRAINING CLASS

- Review of prior Reiki learning and experiences since last course.

- The 3rd level Reiki symbol, origin, meaning and uses.

- Space clearing and creating a healing space with DKM

- Object clearing and blessing

- One Reiki Initiation where the master symbol is placed into the hands.

- Advanced techniques

- Working with the breath

- Time given for hands on practice of all course content

- Manual provided

- Certification

MASTER TEACHER

"Mikao Usui took a torch, and walked up and down the mall where there were thousands of people in the middle of the day. When he was told that he didn't need the torchlight, Usui said, "I am searching for people that need this light to brighten their hearts and cleanse their mind and body."

Hawayo Takata

One of the rewards of teaching Reiki is to observe the positive changes that take place in people over time. Those changes usually affect every aspect of a person's life because Reiki teaches a way of being. The initiation ceremony stirs the seed within someone and the teachings and practices reveal a simple path that if followed may lead them to being called to teach others one day.

In a perfect world they will have embraced Reiki to an extent that they become an example of how effective the Reiki system is and they will naturally draw people to them curious to know more. There are however no rules or perfect ways of being and many paths and ways to connect. The beauty of Reiki is its indiscriminate nature, wanting only the opportunity to flow through someone. People naturally find the right teacher for them and that is good and right. My only requirements when agreeing to teach a master teacher is that they are committed and open hearted, the other skills and requirements that help to make someone a good teacher can be worked upon.

Many Reiki teachers myself included provide a trainee master teacher with an apprenticeship program, whereby the student participates in all levels of Reiki again but in the role of an assistant. This gives valuable experience in holding groups, creating schedules, being flexible, time management, listening skills, exercises and meditations that can be used and dealing with un planned moments. It also provides an opportunity for further note taking and revision of all the Reiki material. I know from experience that every class I teach is slightly different and the more classes a future teacher can attend, the more they will see and learn which will stand them in great stead for when they themselves are teaching. Also we mustn't forget that Reiki is a spiritually guided system of healing for personal spiritual development that is centred on the initiation ceremony.

Having an opportunity to practice this ceremony in real life situations can make the difference in them having the confidence to take that step to being a Reiki master teacher in their own right.

Phyllis Lei Furumoto told an amusing story in Sydney in 1992 about how her Grandmother Hawayo Takata took her to Puerto Rico and told her she was going to be participating in the Reiki training tour.

Hawayo Takata; *"Well you know you're going to have to practice the initiations some more because you are going to work with me."*

Phyllis Furumoto; *"Well, what does that mean, I'm just here to carry your bags."*

Hawayo Takata; *"Oh no, you're here to work with me. I mean why would I pay your plane ticket to Puerto Rico if you weren't going to work with me. I mean you have got to make yourself useful somehow."*

Phyllis Furumoto; *So the next day as we went to the lecture, I just paid attention to what she was saying and really looked at people. She talked about treating someone with cancer and having them have a remission. She talked about somebody who wanted to have a baby, and treating them with Reiki, and then a few months later they got pregnant and so on. I mean just all these incredible stories. We did one class that ran in the afternoons, four afternoons in a row and we did one class that ran in the evenings. She would say, "Watch this person, watch their face. Something is going to change with them." And she would just tell me all these things that would happen, and it was so amazing for me and that was when I first started initiating people.*

As we can see sometimes we learn a great deal from observing a master at work. In the etymology of the kanji characters the character 'Gong' means to master a craft or skill through practice and experience. Assisting your teacher is a valuable way to gain experience, develop your skills and master your own craft.

CHARGING FOR REIKI

I wish to discuss the rather contentious issue of charging money for Reiki. I am not going to advise what you should charge here, but rather discuss the reasons in my opinion why it's a good idea to do so.

I will always remember giving a presentation on Reiki for the first time in Italy many years ago, working through a slightly timid translator. At the end of my presentation I asked if anyone had any questions for me. A lady in the front row wanted to know why Reiki cost so much and why did I feel it was acceptable to charge money for something that was given freely by the Universe. A good question and one that I had an answer for. Unfortunately working through a translator can be challenging and I sat and watched as my translator tried vainly to articulate my answer and was swamped by a crescendo of noise, the room bursting into it's own debate as everyone simultaneously voiced their opinions.

I was left wondering at the time why Reiki seemed to be singled out when it comes to the issue of exchange and why other therapists don't appear to have the same reaction when they ask for money in exchange for their services? It turned out the woman who asked the question gave workshops on dream analysis and I wondered afterwards why she didn't have an issue herself charging for something that was given freely by the universe. We all dream after all don't we?

Fast forward a few months and whilst I was visiting Glastonbury, I saw a notice board offering Reiki training to master level in just a weekend for just £30! I couldn't believe to the degree someone could undervalue Reiki not just in monetary terms but also as a self-development and healing practice. How could someone possibly grasp the depth of Reiki practice to achieve Master level in a weekend?

We can all get pretty stuck around money. Strong feelings and emotions can surface around it and in most surveys on what causes arguments in couples, it comes out on top. But all of these emotions are not actually about money, they are about what we've been taught, assumptions we've made, beliefs, patterns and habits. Money is just the unit of energy exchange. When we step back and look at our attitudes about money, we have an opportunity to see what's driving us—where we're out of balance.

Charging for Reiki is actually a misnomer. The dream analyst was correct when she said the Universe gives Reiki freely. What we charge for is not Reiki, but our time. The cost of a Reiki treatment is usually consistent with the price of a massage in your local area. Reiki practitioners invest time and energy in learning. Reiki training involves both expense and commitment and modern Reiki practitioners have ongoing costs like room rental, equipment, travel expenses, insurance and advertising all of which can be very costly. Reiki practitioners who value themselves charge a fair price for their time, services and commitment to Reiki.

Many people in the Reiki comminity believe it was Hawayo Takata that instilled the belief that we should always charge for a treatment or class. Reiki researcher Elizabeth Latham says

"Takata wanted the Reiki master student to be prepared to either sell their house and in those days $10,000 was the price of a house or pay the equivalent of that price. That been said not everyone paid that amount. Takata used the barter system like a lot of other Reiki masters. Takata was trying to get the expression of worth and commitment from the potential master, that she really really wanted it. This was a Test that Takata asked of the potential master, more than an actual fee. How much were they willing to give of themselves to be a Reiki master? So the $10,000 was a test of Commitment!"

We have to remember it was Dr Usui himself who recognised whilst helping the beggars on the streets of Kyoto that nothing is valued unless there is some form of exchange for it. We know from Hyakuten Inamoto that Chujiro Hayashi charged 50 Yen in 1928 for the Reiki one classes that took place over five days. He would teach a minimum of 10 students at a time which equates to 500 yen, the price at the time of a small house. Reiki two was not for sale. Students exchanging time in Hayashi's clinic for the training.

The 50 yen coin came in different guises and there was a silver 50 yen coin produced as part of the empire collection at that time and fittingly, it was adorned on one side by a pair of Peacocks! I love the fact that this coin may have once been exchanged to learn Reiki with Chujiro Hayashi. Etched upon it are the birds associated with Amida Nyorai and possibly our SHK symbol. These archetypes that in ancient mythology symbolised the transmutation of our lower aspects and our journey to spirit.

50 YEN COIN CIRCA 1926/1928

In terms of our own practice and deciding what value we place upon it, we must remember that it is our personal time we are charging for. As such our fees reflect the value we place on our experience and training. If we find it difficult to ask for money when giving Reiki to people we have to ask ourselves why? Is it because we don't feel good enough to be charging? Do we have a core belief in lack? Do we feel incongruent charging money for something spiritual? Or is it our faith in the practice of Reiki itself that is in question? Maybe our individual practice needs to be worked upon to re install our confidence or maybe we need to go and experience a Reiki treatment from someone else to remind ourselves of Reiki's value again. As Hawayo Takata reiterated when telling the story of Mikao Usui, exchange is an important part of the process. In paying or exchanging for a treatment, a person is investing positively in their own wellbeing and taking personal responsibility, which is self-empowering and reflects an integral sense of personal value.

INITIATIONS

"One cannot give what one does not have. The Reiju and initiation/attunement procedures are methods for sharing the Gift that is the Reiki ability. If you haven't received the Reiki ability yourself, you cannot pass it to another, cannot awaken the ability in another."

James Deacon

The initiations, like the Reiki symbols, have traditionally been kept secret, due to the misconception and fear that if the methods are publically available, the uninitiated may start teaching without having the capacity to do so. I am not going to reveal methods of initiation here, but I will explain the concept, as it is in keeping with the philosophy of this book. What differentiates Reiki from many other healing modalities is the ability to do Reiki is passed like a gift between master and student during the initiation ceremony. For this reason lineages are significant because they legitimize the transmissions being offered. Like a family tree, authentic masters of Reiki can trace their lineage back to Mikao Usui. Reiki itself is seen as the active initiator and like a candle is dormant without a flame, so too a master cannot initiate a student without first having been blessed with the Reiki phenomena themselves. Once initiated, the student is required to use Reiki to both develop a relationship to it and become an effective channel for the energy themselves.

To better understand the mechanics of the initiation process we can view it from the various subtle anatomy models we have explored previously in this book. In fact regardless of which one we look at, there is a consistent idea that a central channel bridging heaven and earth runs through our midpoint. This channel acts as a super highway through which the polarised energies of heaven and earth flow. The Heart Centre found right in the middle of this channel is considered the meeting point and from there energies are distributed throughout our systems. The connection to the earth is realised through the acupoint in the soles of the feet called 'The Bubbling Spring' or Yong Quan. The connection to heaven is realised through the acupoint in the crown called the Bai Hui. In the palms we also have acupoints known as the Lao Gong that allow us to

"Through the initiation we come to the wonderfully simple realisation that we are part of the great universal unfolding"

orchestrate the flow of energy that is emitted through us. The initiating master activates the Reiki phenomenon in the student at these key points and much as a candle is lit by another already with a flame Reiki begins to flow. Once the initiation has taken place, the journey becomes about cultivating a source of energy within. Noticing the manifestation of Reiki inside and allowing it inform what changes need to take place in our lives to allow more room for it to expand. We learn to recognise when it is depleted, when it is abundant and when it is okay to share. It is a mindful journey, of listening, surrendering and allowing our lives to be shaped by its movement until Reiki becomes something that we emanate all around us. Ultimately by allowing ourselves to be an open vessel through which it can flow we are mastered by Reiki and become its loving servant.

A misnomer surrounding Reiki is the idea of temporary initiations. The impression that a Reiki master can temporarily connect you to Reiki but in time the connection will fade away is like saying I am going to give you a holiday at the beach and when you get back you will forget you ever had it. An experience of openness is an experience of openness. The subtle energetic system once awoken to the flow of Reiki is not going to forget the feeling and experience of that. For the subtle energy system this is what it knows, what it was designed for. Certainly if Reiki is not used, like a muscle will weaken, the healing ability will fade somewhat but to suggest the whole experience will return to its previously uninitiated state, is somewhat illogical. I would humbly suggest a short treatment would be just as effective in giving someone an experience of Reiki and far more congruent.

THE MINIMUM CONTENT OF MASTER TEACHER TRAINING CLASS

- Review of prior Reiki learning and experiences since last course.

- Master Initiation

- Learning the Reiki Initiations

- Review of Reiki symbols, origins, meanings and uses.

- Review of content to be covered at each level of Reiki

- Teaching techniques and presentation of content

- Course design

- Charging and fees

- Arrangements made for ongoing mentoring and assisting opportunities

- Information on teaching responsibilities

- Time given for hands on practice of all course content

- Manual provided

- Certification

HONORING HAWAYO TAKATA

"Reiki is a universal force from the Great Divine Spirit. Reiki is not associated with any visible material being, it is an unseen spiritual power that radiates vibration and lifts one into harmony."

Hawayo Takata 1900 – 1980

There is a touching anecdote in Helen J. Harbely's book 'The Hawayo Takata Story' that tells of her birth as the sun rose over the Hawaiian Island of Kauai on Christmas Eve in 1900. Her mother had asked for her to be bathed, wrapped in a blanket and held up to face the rising sun as she named her 'Hawayo' in honor of the newly formed territory of Hawaii. It reminded me of the Sumerian legend earlier in this book where 'Tawsi Melek' The Peacock Angel, after transmitting the breath of life into Adam in the Garden of E-din, turned him to face the sun telling him there was something much greater than he and that praying daily to the sun as a form of the Supreme God would help him to remember this truth. Little was Hawayo Takata's mother to know but destiny had already determined a path for her daughter that would lead her to become entrusted as the caretaker of Reiki by Chujiro Hayashi 40 years later.

She had grown up in Hawaii as a Japanese immigrant, her father working on the sugar cane plantations. Being petite she had struggled with the hard manual labour required in the fields and had found various other jobs splitting her time between teaching the first grade at her boarding school and working in a local store. Later she was to meet the daughter of a wealthy plantation owner that would offer her work as a housekeeper, eventually becoming the head housekeeper. It was here she was to meet her future husband Saichi Takata, the plantation's company bookkeeper. They were very happy and had two daughters but sadly tragedy struck when her husband passed away at the young age of just 34 in October 1930. To support her young family Hawayo Takata had to work hard with little rest and in 1935 started to suffer from ill health herself. This was a difficult time in her life struggling to work with severe abdominal pain and then the sudden passing of one of her sisters. Her parents at the time were in Japan, so she decided to undertake the 4000 mile journey to deliver the sad news of her sister and seek medical help for her increasing poor health.

She travelled by steam ship to Yokohama harbor in Japan and unbeknown to her this was to be the turning point of her life.

View of Pier Yokohama.

YOKOHAMA HARBOR JAPAN

After her sisters memorial in Japan she sought help for her abdominal pain and was diagnosed with a tumour, gallstones and appendicitis. She was admitted into a hospital in Akasaka where she was scheduled to have immediate surgery the following morning and it was there that her profound intuition spoke clearly and loudly leading her towards her life path with Reiki.

Helen J. Haberly writes;

"Mrs. Takata was lying very still on the surgical table eyes closed listening to the splashing of the water and the conversations, when suddenly she heard quite clearly a voice saying, "The operation is not necessary, the operation is not necessary". She opened her eyes and looked around and saw no one speaking, she pinched herself to make sure she was not dreaming and she decided if she heard the voice a third time she would accept it. It was even louder the third time, "The operation is not necessary!" She knew she was awake and sane but what could she do? The voice said, "ask… ask… ask." Whom should she ask? "The head surgeon… the head surgeon… the head surgeon".

The somewhat amusing story is then told of her leaping off the operating table and, in the ensuing chaos, questioning if there was another way to treat her. The head surgeon said he knew of a studio on the other side of town where drugless treatment was being administered and if she had time to spend in Tokyo he could direct her towards it.

After Mikao Usui's Death, Chujiro Hayashi had started a small clinic in Tokyo named "Hayashi Reiki Kenkyu-kai". He trained students who then served their apprenticeship in his studio working in pairs on patients to maximise the energy flow. There was anything up to sixteen practitioners treating eight patients at any one time all supervised by Chujiro Hayashi. It was to this clinic that Hawayo Takata had been directed by the head surgeon at Akasaka hospital to cure her of a tumour, gallstones and appendicitis.

Throughout her treatment Hawayo Takata became fascinated with Reiki and wished to learn how to do it herself. At the time, Reiki was strictly guarded and Hayashi was adamant that it be kept that way. NO advertising or publicity of any kind was permitted. This was possibly due to a decree being issued by the Shinto Shrine in 1873 prohibiting any forms of spiritual shamanism to practice without a license. The Shinto Shrine also controlled all aspects of training and competence in the traditional ways of Shamanism. So healing practices like Reiki had to remain hidden for fear of reprisals, as they were considered by the authorities as nothing more than witchcraft.

However Hawayo Takata was determined and it is said she canvassed the help of the head surgeon who had originally directed her to the clinic to persuade Chujiro Hayashi to teach her. He apparently was so impressed that he agreed. After just four months Hawayo Takata had seen a complete recovery in her own health and within six months had decided to remain in Japan to work in the Hayashi Clinic. It is perhaps here that we need to appreciate the relationship Hawayo Takata had with Chujiro Hayashi and his wife. She accepted their invitation to live in the Hayashi family home for the duration of her Reiki practitioner training and served a one-year apprenticeship with him in Japan. She would work in the clinic every morning for five hours and often accompany Chujiro Hayashi making house calls in the afternoon. This daily mentoring alongside Hayashi gave her an incredible depth and breadth of hands on experience working with Reiki and at the end of the year she was given her second degree initiation.

Hawayo Takata returned to Hawaii in the summer of 1937 and set up a treatment practice in Kapaa on Kauai Island. On 24th September 1937 Chujiro Hayashi accompanied by his daughter Kiyoe Hayashi left for Hawaii from Yokohama Japan. A journey he undertook to entrust Reiki into Hawayo Takata's capable hands for safekeeping lest it became lost forever during the second world war. He remained in Hawaii for nearly 4 months making the return journey on the 22nd of February 1938. Below is the ships log showing entries for him and his daughter.

I have zoomed in here in the hope that you can make out next to Chujiro Hayashi's name it states he is master of 'Hayashi Reiki Kenkyu'. Written by hand underneath, it say's 'Spiritual Healer'.

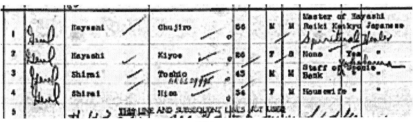

THE PHOTOGRAPH BELOW HAS NEVER
BEEN PUBLISHED IN ITS ENTIRETY UN-CROPPED.

In the photograph we see Hawayo Takata demonstrating to a class of over 100 students in late 1937 early 1938. Chujiro Hayashi is sitting to her left in the row behind her with his daughter. We can see the Reiki principles hanging on a notice board behind him to his left. The white kanji characters across the bottom of the print read 'Reiki Treatment Training Meeting At The Young Buddhist Association'. This unique unedited photograph illustrates to me how highly he regarded Hawayo Takata. Below is a cropped version of the picture to give more detail.

In 2013 James Deacon wrote on his web site with regard the photograph,

"I feel that, for the Reiki community at large, this photo is important in that (particularly in the current climate where some factions of the Reiki community are seemingly intent on attempting to discredit, or at very least play down the importance and validity of, Takata-sensei's training,) it provides valuable 'supporting evidence' pertaining to Chujiro Hayashi's ongoing association with, and post-apprenticeship (or rather 'post-graduation') mentoring and support of, Hawayo Takata in her quest to bring Reiki Ryoho to the western world".

Let us put ourselves in Chujiro Hayashi's position for a moment. He came from a significant high-class Samurai family with friends and contacts in high places. He was aware of the possibility of war between Japan and the USA. Imagine him choosing to undertake a round trip by ship of nearly 8000 miles to make Hawayo Takata the custodian of Hayashi Reiki Kenkyu [his system], but only offer her a watered down version of it? What sense would that make? If his concern were that Reiki could be lost in Japan through the war then to give her an incomplete or simplified practice defies logic. I absolutely believe he would have ensured the system, understanding, knowledge, practices and energetic link back to Mikao Usui was transferred in its entirety and intact!

HAWAYO TAKATA AND
CHUJIRO HAYASHI
YEAR 1937 IN HAWAII

The following photograph not published before shows Hawayo Takata in 1938 with her students after Chujiro Hayashi had returned to Japan confirming that she was teaching Reiki prior to the onset of war. Once again we can see the Reiki principles on the back wall. Hawayo Takata is fifth from the readers left and five rows back. The appearance of children in the photograph supports Hawayo Takata's stance of 'Family first'.

A few years after this photograph was taken, it is said Hawayo Takata had a vivid dream of Chujiro Hayashi wearing a formal kimono of white silk and, sensing something was wrong, decided to set sail for Japan in March 1940. Her intuition proved correct and upon her arrival she was to learn from Mrs Hayashi that her husband had planned to take his own life but had not yet set the date. It is said that upon his return to Japan from Hawaii, Chujiro Hayashi had been under pressure to take up another Naval Command. This caused him great consternation due to the conflict between his call to duty as Japan entered into the Second World War and the healing principles learnt through his practice of Reiki. If Hayashi refused he would have likely been considered a traitor. Being from high class Samurai ancestry and not wanting to bring dishonour to his family name, he decided on May 11th 1940 in the presence of his wife, Hawayo Takata, students and friends to commit Seppuku [ritual suicide] at his summer Villa in Atami near Mt Fuji.

During breakfast on the day of his transition Chujiro Hayashi told Hawayo Takata that his family had decided she was the person to take over his work. Hayashi's wife wanted to retire to the country home and did not have the willingness to carry on teaching Reiki by herself, his daughter was married and didn't wish to work and his son wanted to run his own business. So he entrusted his Reiki system completely to her including his Tokyo home and clinic. At one o'clock it is reported, Hayashi entered the room where all the guests were gathered dressed in the same white silk kimono Hawayo Takata had seen in her dream. He calmly explained his motives and then took his own life. He was sixty-two years of age.

Early descriptions of Chujiro Hayashi death tell of him sitting in meditation and stopping his own heart or simply leaving his body. It would have been extremely amazing if he could have simply sat in meditation and willed his own heart to stop. I believe it is highly likely that Hawayo Takata was extremely conscious of the anti- Japanese sentiment at the time and the concept of her teacher committing Hara Kiri did nothing to support her cause. It would have been impolite to speak of Seppuku publically, especially in the west, hence her story.

Reiki researcher Elizabeth Latham say's

"The Seppuku is a "highly implied" traditional Samurai ritual act in Takatas's story. Such as the white silk kimono, the ceremony with invited guests, as witness's, the timing of the event, the ceremony of the last dinner and the three arteries equals the three belly cuts in the ritual."

Elizabeth Latham managed to obtain from the Yasakuni Shrine a letter which confirms Chujiro Hayashi died by self determination.

Ref: 698, 9 September 2014

To: Elizabeth M Latham

From: Research Section, General Affairs Department, Yasukuni Jinjya

Re: research on deceased estate (reply)

With regard to your enquiry about Chujiro Hayashi, Navy Colonel, we wish to confirm that Yasukuni Shrine has no information as deceased (i.e. enshrined person).

The reasons for not having any record is that Colonel Hayashi already retired from the Navy during the Taisho period (i.e. from July 30, 1912, to December 25, 1926) and that he was not a member of the military personnel when he passed away.

It is also understood that suicide by sword was the cause of the death and the death was not directly related to the war, so these are the reasons why we do not hold information on the deceased.

靖調第六九八号

平成二十六年九月九日

　　　　　　　　　　　　　　　　靖　國　神　社　祭　務　部　調　査　課

Elizabeth M Latham　殿

　　　　　死没者関調査に関する件　（回答）

首標の件、このたび御問合せ戴きました林忠次郎海軍大佐につきましては、靖國神社には御祭神としての情報はございません。

記録が無い理由として、履歴から林大佐は大正時代には既に海軍を退役しており、死没時には軍人ではなかったこと。また死没の原因が自刃となっており、その死が戦役に直接関係していないことが理由であろうと考えられます。

以上、甚だ略で御座いますが回答と致します。

　　　　　　　　　　　　　　　　　　　　　　　　　　　　　　　　　　　以　上

The word Reiki has become synonymous with Hawayo Takata through the teachings of Chujiro Hayashi. As we have seen, Hawayo Takata learnt Reiki directly from Chujiro Hayashi, serving her apprenticeship at his clinic and receiving not only the master level attunement directly from him but also his blessing and it was to her he entrusted his Reiki system and clinic. Since then many other hands on healing systems have adopted the name Reiki whilst claiming to be in possession of a more original system or openly admitting they have changed the content. But it was Reiki as taught by Hawayo Takata that became famous throughout the world.

The 'Usui Reiki Ryoho' that Hawayo Takata made so successful is often referred to in the present climate, as 'Western Reiki' and it would be understandable if many in the Reiki community felt offended by this label. The message Hawayo Takata left for us was *"Reiki is Gods plan. To free ourselves from ignorance, to live in harmony with ourself and others, to love all beings."* My understanding of Reiki is that it has no divisions.

CONCLUSION

"Our soul is not contained within the limits of our physical body but rather our physical body is contained within the limitlessness of our soul ".

Jim Carey

In the summer of 1983, at the tender age of eighteen, I was at Art College studying photography. At the weekends I would ride my rusty old bicycle to the train station and head off to Oxford to see friends. One weekend a good friend wanted to see a fortune-teller that was at the market every Saturday morning. We had to take something belonging to us that she would use as a proxy to read our energy. I grudgingly went along with it, my head at the time far more troubled with other matters than having my fortune read! When we arrived in the busy market, there was a small crowd gathered around this woman sitting under an awning on a white plastic garden chair. She had a face that looked lived in and tanned hands. The Kindness in her eyes belied a penetrating look and there was a gentle knowing about her. My friend was ushered forward to sit down and as her reading began, I drifted into my own little reverie, my mind composing pictures with the shapes, light and colours of the market. I don't know how long I drifted but something pulled me back to the present and I was aware the fortune-teller was looking at me and beckoning me to sit, having now finished with my friend. I handed her a bracelet I wore all the time, but something inside of me told me she didn't really need it, it was just part of the performance. She looked straight into my eyes and said "You are a very private person and would prefer not to be doing this in public." True I thought, in fact I would prefer not to be doing this at all. I don't remember much of what she said to me and cannot remember how long I was there, but at the very end she took my hands in hers and looked straight at me and said something that has remained with me ever since. She said,

"The world is not as bad a place as you think it is. I am giving this to you as a gift, so that you will remember this moment and know there are good people here on earth".

I know now that it was a course correction in my life, a moment where I was truly seen by another human being and it touched me so deeply that I never forgot it. As John Milton wrote in Paradise Lost, "The mind is its own place, and in itself can make a heaven of hell and a hell of heaven". Prior to meeting that wonderful little gypsy angel in the market, I was beginning to create hell for myself and I could no longer see the good in the world until she saw my pain and reached out to me. A small moment of Kindness that altered my whole way of being.

THE STARFISH STORY.

"AN OLD MAN WALKING ON THE BEACH AFTER A STORM.

IN THE DISTANCE HE COULD SEE SOMEONE MOVING LIKE A DANCER.

AS HE CAME CLOSER, HE SAW THAT IT WAS A YOUNG WOMAN PICKING UP STARFISH AND GENTLY THROWING THEM BACK INTO THE OCEAN.

"YOUNG LADY, WHY ARE YOU THROWING STARFISH INTO THE OCEAN?"

"THE TIDE IS GOING OUT AND IF I DO NOT THROW THEM IN, THEY WILL DIE," SHE SAID

"BUT YOUNG LADY DO YOU NOT REALISE THAT THERE ARE MANY MILES OF BEACH AND THOUSANDS OF STARFISH? YOU CANNOT POSSIBLY MAKE A DIFFERENCE."

THE YOUNG WOMAN LISTEN POLITELY, THEN BENT DOWN, PICKED UP ANOTHER STARFISH AND THREW IT INTO THE SEA. "IT MADE A DIFFERENCE FOR THAT ONE" SHE SAID.

If I have learnt one thing through Reiki, it is that there is no division, no separation anywhere other than the separation we create within our minds. Your pain is my pain; your joy my joy. And yet as humans we so often choose to sleep in the illusion of separateness, unaware and distracted by the dramas and stories that surround us.

Every day newsstands preach sectarianism, discrimination and hatred. Attaching importance to perceived differences between subdivisions. Stories of suffering, poverty, famine, violence and terrorism broadcast right into our living rooms. It is as if the world has become a living hell and yet if you ask people what they most want, they will answer Peace! The only place where we can find peace is within the silence of our own hearts. When we do, we understand that it is all that truly matters. Our sense of community our care for others is fuelled by the love fostered in the heart. Separation instead is driven by fear and to exclude anything in our universe is not an act of love but of fear.

Sadly fear has become an epidemic of global proportions and to what cost for the future generations? A heart allowed to harden by anger and worry becomes limited in its capacity to love. When eyes lose their sparkle we are seeing the soul retreat, and as the trance is deepened the belief that the world is not safe is held to be real. But it is all just smoke and mirrors hiding the truth.

Reiki is a call from the very heart of our universe, it is a call to return home, to reconnect and awaken to reality. If we listen, we come to realise that there is no separation, no them and us, no external God... Our planet and everything upon it, is a creative expression of one self. We are a cherished part, interconnected with everything else, like a fisherman is as connected to the ocean into which he casts his line, as he is to the fish he hopes to catch. Reiki's defining message tells how intimately the fabric of the universe is interwoven and through its subtle flow, helps us access a sense of completeness.

The difficulty in trying to conclude this book is that deep down I know there is no conclusion. The thread that I have followed forms just a small part of an evolving and expanding tapestry, enriched by the contributions of masters and practitioners throughout the world. This is my interpretation and to date my understanding of the system I have grown to love.

When I embarked upon the journey to write this book I wasn't completely sure where it would take me. I heard a calling and decided to heed the call. Following the thread that has weaved its way through the days and months inspiring me to look here, read this, go there. I have at times been amazed by what has unfolded. It is with some trepidation that I publish what I have found. My hope is, that you the reader will appreciate the open sense of curiosity and wonder that has marked my intent.

Through writing this book I have developed a deep appreciation for the principle caretakers of Reiki, Chujiro Hayashi and Hawayo Takata. I have come to see the genius of Mikao Usui and I hope to have revealed a little of his astute wisdom and understanding. Through his experience on Mount Kurama he was awakened to the realisation that it was the birth right of every man and woman to stand tall between heaven and earth. The map he left was his contribution to the rest of humanity to help each and every one of us transform our lower earthbound selves, awaken to reality and acknowledge the full beauty and splendor of being one with the universe.

"THE ORIGIN OF ALL, THE ESSENCE OF
OUR BEING IS PURE CONSCIOUSNESS."

ABOUT THE AUTHOR

Richard Ellis is the author of two further books on Reiki and a complementary health practitioner specialising in the relationship between mind and body. He is a teacher of Reiki, a clinical Hypnotherapist, NLP practitioner and a teacher of 5 element Qigong.

Richard's career in complementary therapy began in the early 1990's completing his training as a Reiki instructor by early 1995. He then continued to work alongside his teacher June Woods, whilst living at the Findhorn Foundation in Scotland. Following a period of travel and international teaching, he was approached to write his first book 'Empower your life with Reiki' published by Hodder & Stoughton in 1999. This book was published in the United States by Sterling Publishing and re-titled 'Practical Reiki' and went on to be translated into several languages.

Following the success of Practical Reiki, he started work on his second book 'Reiki and the Seven Chakras' published in 2002 by Vermillion and has been translated into several languages.

His keen interest in the chakra system, the nature of disease and the link between mind and body, has led him to develop his own training program utilizing posture analysis and non verbal communication called 'The Body Never Lies'.

Richard Ellis runs his healing practice from East Dorset England where he lives with his family.

Other books by Richard Ellis

Empower Your Life With Reiki (Hodder & Stoughton UK Edition)
Practical Reiki (Sterling Publishing US Edition)
Reiki and The Seven Chakras (Vermillion)

To contact the Author visit:

www.practicalreiki.com

BIBLIOGRAPHY

A Brief History of Qi *Zhang Yu Huan & Ken Rose*

Codex Nuttall – [Manuscript on the Swastika] *Zelia Nuttall anthropologist*

Hawayo Takata's essay and original voice recordings *Elizabeth Latham*

Hawayo Takata Story *Helen J.Haberly*

Introduction To The Shogua *Stephen Karcher Ph.D*

onmarkproductions.com

Prophets Of Peace *Robert Kisala*

Reiki's birthplace *Jessica Miller*

Reiki Pages www.aetw.org *James Deacon*

Reiki The True Story *Don Beckett*

Reiki 2nd level Booklet *Mary Mcfayden*

Shamanism and Qigong *Jim Haynes*

Shaolin Qi Gong *Shi Xinggui*

Soul Healing Miracles *Dr Zhi Gang Sha*

Tantric Buddhism in East Asia' *Richard K Payne*

The Web Has No Weaver *Ted J Kaptchuk OMD*

The Story Of Malek Taus www.thepixelatedpen.com *Paige Pixel*

The International Institute for Reiki Training *Lawrence Ellyard*

Transcripts of stories from Sydney in 1992 *Phyllis Lei Furumoto*

Vital Breath Of The Dao *Zhongxian Wu*

www.thedaoofdragonball.com 'Genki Darma'

www.en.wiktionary.org/wiki/雨 'Rei'

www.jayarava.blogspot.co.uk 'Seed syllable of Great Compassion'

http://www.thehinduforum.com 'Peacock Deities'

www.khadrochineitsang.com 'School Of Chi Nei Tsang'

www.sourcememory.net 'Woman Shaman'

www.visiblemantra.org 'Hrih'

www.wildmind.org 'Hrih Mantra'

www.yeziditruth.org/the_peacock_angel

13172251R00141

Printed in Great Britain
by Amazon.co.uk, Ltd.,
Marston Gate.